# Lies Told in the Bible

Intriguing Stories of Lies and Consequences

Patricia Von Johnson

All rights reserved.

This book is protected by the copyright laws of the
United States of America.

This book may not be copied or reprinted
for commercial gain or profit.
The use of short quotations or occasional page copying for
personal or group study is permitted and encouraged.
Permission will be granted upon request.

Scripture quotations are taken from
THE HOLY BIBLE,
NEW INTERNATIONAL VERSION®, NIV®
Copyright © 1973, 1978, 1984, 2011 by Biblica, Inc.™
Used by permission. All rights reserved worldwide.

Published by Suncoast Digital Press, Inc., October 2019
Sarasota Florida
www.suncoastdigitalpress.com

Lies Told in the Bible copyright © 2016, 2019 by
Patricia Von Johnson

ISBN 978-1-939237-70-5

Library of Congress Control Number: 2019912263

Cover Design By: Patricia Von Johnson and Christiana Emmanuel
Editor: Angela R. Shears

# Dedication

To the only wise God
Who says to give
Honor to whom it is due.
I give You total Honor as
You provided me the vision,
instruction, and dialogue
for this book,
from cover to back
in its entirety.
I was the first
to repent in tears.
I am grateful.

# *Praise for* Lies Told in the Bible: Intriguing Stories of Lies and Consequences

"**Lies Told in the Bible** is phenomenal! It is an encyclopedic work that can be used by Sunday school classes for weekly discussions, as well as by families for devotional discussions. Outstanding work!"

-**Dr Gary Cohen.** Professor of Biblical Studies, Trinity International University, Temple University of Philadelphia, science major, BSed Faith Theological Seminary, Mdiv, STM, ThD from Grace Theological Seminary, Winona Lake, IN. LittD conferred writings include, Hosea - Amos, and Understanding Revelation. D.D. Degree from South Florida Bible College and Theological Seminary. His book, *Revelation Visualized*, with Salem Kirban, was recently reprinted by AMG. Dr Cohen was an Army Reserve Chaplain (COL) and graduate of the USAF Air War College. He holds a commercial pilots license and advanced ground instructor certificate.

"I praise God for your diligence in writing this book and in carefully focusing a study of the Bible on lies and lying. You have provided a great overview on the topic of lying as revealed in the Bible. Your book is a great expanded concordance on learning what the Bible says about lying."

-**Dr Norman R. Wise.** Executive Director of Living Water Counseling Center, Geneva College, Geneva Falls, Pennsylvania. Bachelor of Arts in Biblical Theology and Bachelor of Science in Education, Knox Theological Seminary, Fort Lauderdale, FL. Masters of Divinity and Doctorate of Ministry. Adjunct professor at Knox Theological Seminary, Fort Lauderdale, FL and Reformed Theological Seminary, Boca Branch, Coral Ridge Presbyterian Church, Fort Lauderdale, FL, Minister of Discipleship. Co-authored four books with Dr James Kennedy. First Church West, Tamarac, FL, Senior Pastor.

# Acknowledgments

I'd like to first thank my incredible editor Angela Rickabaugh Shears whose professional contributions to my book are priceless; appropriately esteemed a blessing.

I want to acknowledge Barbara Dee and her team at Suncoast Digital Press for the attention to detail, encouragement, and final publication of this book.

Also, special thanks to Dr. Gary G. Cohen and Dr. Norm Wise for their valuable feedback on my original draft.

I'd like to honorably acknowledge my parents—my father, Minor, and my mother, Marjorie. Wanda, Lyn, and Margie, thank you for being supportive sisters.

To my daughter, Qiana, "I love you."

# Contents

Preface — xi

*Chapter 1*
Lies Told in Genesis — 1

*Chapter 2*
Lies Told in Exodus — 15

*Chapter 3*
Lies Told in Leviticus — 23

*Chapter 4*
Lies Told in Numbers — 27

*Chapter 5*
Lies Told in Joshua — 31

*Chapter 6*
Lies Told in Judges — 35

*Chapter 7*
Lies Told in 1 Samuel — 39

*Chapter 8*
Lies Told in 2 Samuel — 45

*Chapter 9*
Lies Told in 1 Kings — 53

*Chapter 10*
Lies Told in 2 Kings — 59

*Chapter 11*
Lies Told in 2 Chronicles — 63

*Chapter 12*
Lies Told in Nehemiah — 67

*Chapter 13*
Liars in Job — 71

| | |
|---|---|
| *Chapter 14* <br> Mentions in Psalms | *75* |
| *Chapter 15* <br> Mentions in Proverbs | *79* |
| *Chapter 16* <br> Lies Told in Isaiah | *83* |
| *Chapter 17* <br> Lies Told in Jeremiah | *87* |
| *Chapter 18* <br> Lies Told in Matthew | *93* |
| *Chapter 19* <br> Lies Told in Mark | *99* |
| *Chapter 20* <br> Lies Told in Luke | *103* |
| *Chapter 21* <br> Lies Told in John | *107* |
| *Chapter 22* <br> Lies Told in Acts | *113* |
| *Chapter 23* <br> Lies Told in 2 Corinthians | *119* |
| Afterword | *122* |
| Appendix | *135* |
| About the Author | *139* |

# Preface

Rehab lied. Her lie saved lives, including her own. There were consequences. The nature and motive of her lie determined the consequences. (More about Rehab's story is found in Chapter 5 of this book and in the Bible's Book of Joshua.)

Let's bring the issue of lying current. If an elementary school teacher encountered a pedophile—who at gunpoint asked which classroom was filled with young children—and the teacher lied and actually led him to where the school's security guard was located, her lie's consequence averted tragedy, based on its nature and motive.

Adversely, lies with wicked or malicious motives get equally wicked or malicious consequences as well. Wicked lies uncoil and clobber, whether immediately, after a decade, or even a lifetime later. The course of a lie is ultimately exposure, and liars will not escape from their lies. The truth is more powerful than lies; just as God, who is The Truth, is more powerful than Satan, the father of lies. Many have erroneously believed that "the truth hurts." That commonly coined phrase deceives humankind into devaluing truth.

God says the truth will set us free. Lies hurt and deceive—they hold people in bondage.

The power of the tongue is not to be taken lightly. The intent of a lie spoken is actualized in the person speaking it. In the Bible, lies with wicked intentions generally brought like results to the liar. Lies to cause harm, generally brought harm on the liar. Lies told to help, brought help, when help was its truthful intent. The true and living God, who commands us not to lie, knows the true intent of our words, as He knows our hearts. Some are fooled by lies, never God. In the Book of Proverbs, it states that simple-minded people believe anything **(Proverbs 14:15)**. Wise people think of the actions; we must consider what the person's actions are also "saying."

I display the lies told in the Bible with a synopsis of what occurred amid the lie. I am simply just the messenger. The Bible states the devil is the father of lies **(John 8:44);** we must not be pawns or peddlers of his offspring. Yes, it is that extreme-an intentional hurtful lie is from the one whose sole purpose is your destruction. Our lies empower the devil's efforts.

In **1 Kings 13:18** (chapter 13, verse 18), a prophet downright lied and the Bible expressly states so. Many others in the Bible also lied. Sometimes God has allowed a lying spirit, but for a great purpose-always against wickedness.

All Scripture in this book is taken from the **New International Version (NIV)** of the Bible. And all Scripture herein is printed using bold and italic emphases. After reading each story, I urge you to consult the entire chapter in the Bible to seek the whole truth of the matter. It is best to read each story's conclusion with clarity. These historical stories are amazing page-turners—when you understand them.

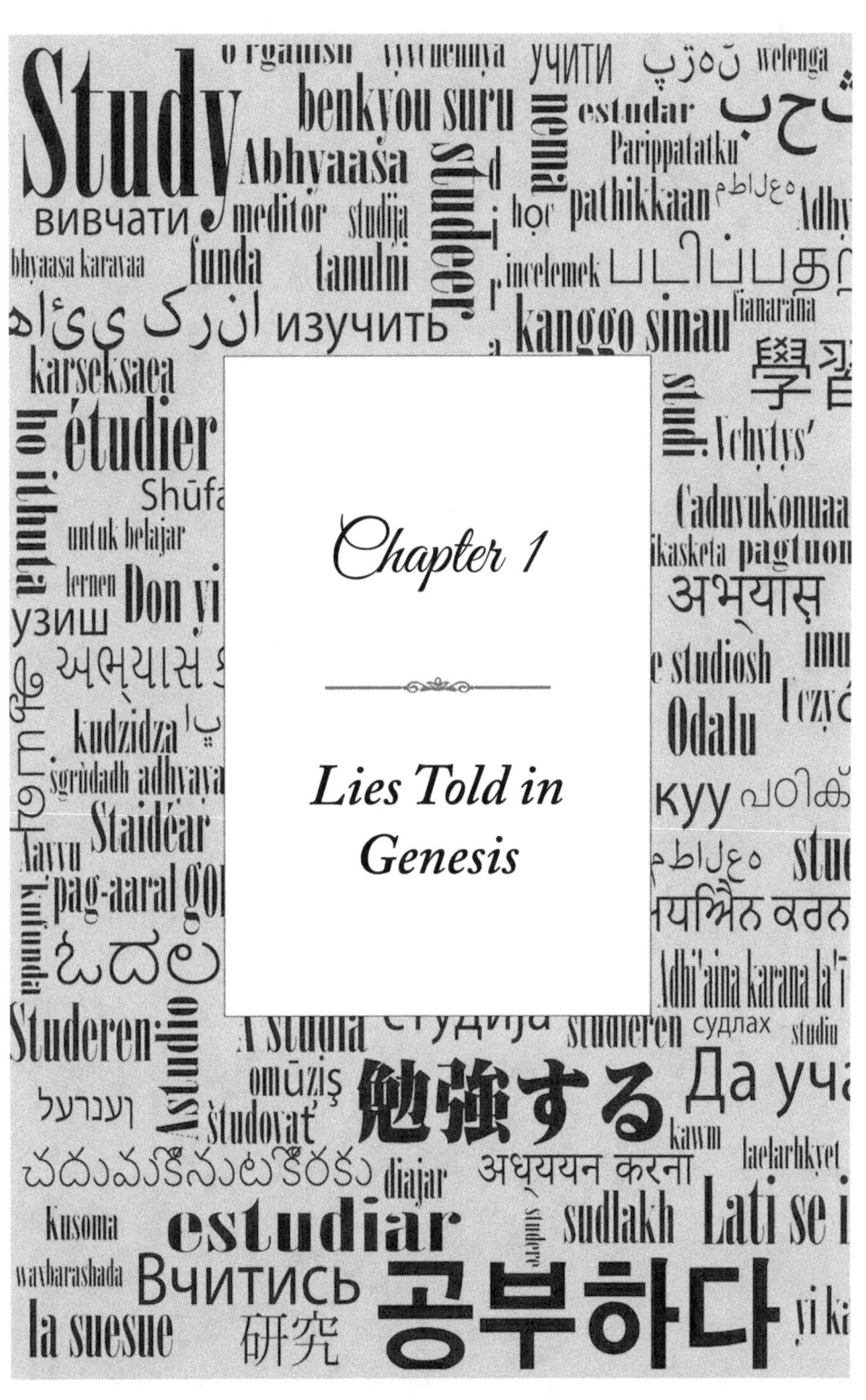

# Chapter 1

## Lies Told in Genesis

Satan's Lie: The culprit of the first lie is the father of lies. Satan lies to the woman Eve, in the Garden of Eden. **Genesis 3:4:** *"'You will not certainly die,' the serpent said to the woman."* God clearly states in prior Scripture (Genesis 2:15-17) that Adam and Eve were neither to eat of nor touch the tree of the knowledge of good and evil or they would die. This lie altered humankind forever. The power of one lie till this day continues to alter lives with the expressed purpose of Satan, its originator, to steal, kill, and destroy (see John 10:10).

---

Cain's Lie: The first murder—Cain kills his brother, Abel; their parents were Adam and Eve. **Genesis 4:9:** *"Then the Lord said to Cain, 'Where is your brother Abel?' 'I don't know,' he replied. 'Am I my brother's keeper?'"* Cain lied to God—he had, in fact, just killed Abel in a fit of anger. If you believe God is who He says He is, why bother lying to the God who knows all? It is futile. Equally questionable is lying to yourself.

---

Abram's Lie: Abram (later called Abraham) lied to protect himself from possible death while traveling with his family. His wife was so beautiful, Abram asked her to tell the Egyptians she was his sister, or they would kill him to take her. **Genesis 12:13:** *"Say you are my sister, so that I will be treated well for your sake and my life will be spared because of you."* When Pharaoh took Abram's wife, God plagued Pharaoh and his house with great plagues. God intervened on Abram's behalf in accordance to his motive for lying. Pharaoh called Abram and asked why he failed to reveal that Sarah was his wife—not his sister—as Pharaoh was planning to possibly marry her. Abram, his wife, and all they owned were freely sent away, unharmed, because God intervened. When Abram lied, he did not do so with wicked motives or intent, therefore he received like consequences.

---

Sarah's Lie: Is there anything too hard for God? No. Abraham and Sarah were of old age when God said Sarah would birth a son. Sarah laughed at the notion that she, well past child-bearing age, could birth a child. She thought of her own abilities instead of believing in the God with whom all things are possible. If God says it—it is truth. Her laughter was simply doubt. **Genesis 18:15: *"Sarah was afraid, so she lied and said, 'I did not laugh.' But he said, 'Yes, you did laugh.'"*** God exposed her lie. God always exposes lies.

---

Lot's Daughter's Lie: God destroyed the sin-filled cities of Sodom and Gomorrah. Lot and his daughters were spared and went to live in the city named Zoar. **Genesis 19:31: *"One day the older daughter said to the younger, 'Our father is old, and there is no man around here to give us children—as is the custom all over the earth.'"*** Lot's oldest daughter lied to justify her wickedly selfish intentions. There were and would be many men from Lot, who was of Abraham's same seed—God told Abraham that his descendants would be as numerous as the stars (Exodus 32:13). Both daughters got their father drunk and had sexual relations with him. This lie produced the birth of Moab, the father of Moabites, and Ben-Ammi, the father of the Ammonites. Consequently, the people who came from these unions were rebellious and served false gods.

---

> *Throughout history, innumerable lies have ruined relationships even unto death - simply because of the extreme beauty of a woman.*

Abraham's Lie: Now Abraham journeyed on to the south country where Abimelech was king. **Genesis 20:2:** ***"and there Abraham said of his wife Sarah, 'She is my sister.' Then Abimelech king of Gerar sent for Sarah and took her."*** Abraham was a great man of faith, yet he did not learn from the first experience of lying, saying his wife Sarah was his sister. But, God once again intervened on Abraham's behalf accordingly. God and His Word is the same yesterday, now, and forevermore. In a dream God warned King Abimelech that he was marked for death if he took another man's wife. God also told the king that He knew he was acting with integrity and was innocent, thinking that Sarah was unmarried. For this reason, God kept King Abimelech from having sexual relations with Sarah.

God is no respecter of persons—He shows no favoritism. Not just kings, but every individual who lives with integrity will receive protection from lies, whether warned in dreams, hints or hunches, even a stirring in our conscience. We must not ignore these warning signs. God instructed Abimelech to give Sarah back to Abraham, for Abraham was a prophet, and his purpose would be fulfilled.

God does not withdraw His purpose or gifts He gives us. When we sin, it is we ourselves who tarnish our own purpose and gifts. Abraham suffered numerous circumstances to foil perceived problems due to his wife's extreme beauty. Throughout history, innumerable lies have ruined relationships even to death—simply because of the extreme beauty of a woman.

---

Isaac's Lie: Like father, like son. Isaac also chose to lie, saying that his wife Rebekah is his sister. He lied for the exact reason his father lied— his wife's beauty. **Genesis 26:7:** *"When the men of that place asked him about his wife, he said, 'She is my sister,' because he was afraid to say, 'She is my wife.' He thought, 'The men of this place might kill me on account of Rebekah, because she is beautiful.'"* Sometime later the king of the Philistines looked from his window and saw Isaac and Rebekah in an intimate act; and he called Isaac and asked why he lied, putting others in jeopardy of guilt as someone may have taken Rebekah sexually. The Philistine knew Isaac was a man of God. And he also knew there was a price to pay when you take another's spouse. The king ordered all of his people not to harm Isaac or Rebekah, or the offender would surely be put to death.

---

Jacob's Lie: God blessed Isaac and he lived in abundance for many years. He was now very old, nearly blind, and near death. Before dying, Isaac wanted to bless his oldest son Esau. His wife and younger son Jacob plotted that Jacob would receive the blessing instead of Esau. **Genesis 27:19:** *"Jacob said to his father, 'I am Esau your firstborn. I have done as you told me. Please sit up and eat some of my game, so that you may give me your blessing.'"* Jacob lied to receive his brother's blessing. And he continued to lie—lies are generally followed by more lies in succession.

This is typical of a lie, trying to perpetrate truth, to no avail.

Isaac sent Jacob, pretending to be Esau, to the field to get food for his meal before he died. **Genesis 27:20:** *"Isaac asked his son, 'How did you find it so quickly, my son?' 'The Lord your God gave me success,' he replied."* This time Jacob lied using God. His father could hear that this son's voice sounded differently, but due to touching Jacob's "hairy" hand, Isaac accepted the lie. Esau was very hairy, and part of the plot was to make Jacob appear hairy using animal skins; they knew the blind see through touch, and Isaac would surely touch his son. Isaac believed Jacob was Esau and blessed him (Genesis 27:27-29). The cycle of lies continued.

**Genesis 27:24:** *"'Are you really my son Esau?' he asked. 'I am,' he replied."* Jacob lied to his father. He and his mother were wholly aware of the power the father has to speak blessings or curses over the lives of their children. This power still exists within fathers today, whether they are aware or not. Many have haphazardly spoken curses over their children by simply telling them, "You will never amount to anything." Even the poorest father can speak great blessings on their children's lives and change the family dynamics with the power of the tongue. The power was not due to Isaac's wealth, but his position as father.

---

Rachel's Lie: Jacob married Leah, and then he married Rachel. In secret, they left on the journey to return to Jacob's people, not telling the women's father, Laban. When Laban became aware of their departure, he cursed Jacob in anger, partly because his images of false gods had been stolen. His daughter Rachel had stolen them.

Laban caught up with Jacob and his family and searched every tent for his stolen items. Rachel used a lie that continues to be used by women today, for various reasons. She lied saying she was unable to stand and greet him because of her menstrual period. She was actually sitting on the furniture under which she had hidden the stolen items. Laban believed her, and therefore did not find the items. **Genesis 31:35:** *"Rachel said to her father, 'Don't be angry, my lord, that I cannot stand up in your presence; I'm having my period.' So he searched but could not find the household gods."*

Do you think Rachel was free of the consequence of her lie because she was not caught immediately?

---

Jacob's Sons' Lie: Jacob's daughter Dinah was raped by the king's son, Shechem. Shechem longed for her and wanted to marry her. The molestation was unacceptable, as was marriage to the uncircumcised (non-Jew) unacceptable in Israel. This was double disgrace. King Hamor asked Jacob to give his daughter to his son in marriage and allow their people to intermarry. He offered to give them everything they wanted as dowry for the marriage. The sons of Jacob, Dinah's brothers, answered deceitfully; they lied in an effort to plot revenge for Dinah's rape. Jacob's sons told Shechem and Hamor that they could not give their sister to an uncircumcised man. Under their law all men were to be circumcised. **Genesis 34:15-17:** *"We will enter into an agreement with you on one condition only: that you become like us by circumcising all your males. Then we will give you our daughters and take your daughters for ourselves. We'll settle among you and become one people with you. But if you will not agree to be circumcised, we'll take our sister and go.'"* Hamor and Shechem consented, thinking they would marry. They had each and every one of their men circumcised. After three days when all the men were sore and incapacitated, Jacob's sons went to the city and killed every male. They also killed Hamor and Shechem and took their sister from them. They had defiled their sister, and this was their revenge.

Jacob had not consented to his son's actions and said to Simeon and Levi that other cities would come against him and destroy all that was his. He said their revenge would be reciprocated with further revenge. Jacob's sons, Dinah's brothers, replied, asking if their sister should be treated like a prostitute. Jacob had his entire household put away their strange gods, and he took away their images and hid them. Therefore, God protected them as they journeyed. The terror of God was on the cities they passed, and no one pursued Jacob's family.

Jacob's youngest and most favored son Joseph was envied by his older brothers. Joseph dreamed a prophecy that all of his family would one day bow down to him. His father accepted the prophecy, but his half- brothers grew more envious and hated Joseph. The brothers went out into the field to tend to the animals. After a time, Jacob sent Joseph to see if his brothers were well and in need of anything. When they saw Joseph approaching, they plotted to kill him. **Genesis 37:20:** *"Come now, let's kill him and throw him into one of these cisterns and say that a ferocious animal devoured him. Then we'll see what comes of his dreams."* Reuben told them not to kill Joseph, but rather put him in a pit out in the wilderness. He wanted his brother to eventually make it back to their father.

His brothers put Joseph in an empty pit with no water. Then they thought it would be more profitable to sell him into slavery. This took place without Reuben's knowledge; and when he went back to the pit to get Joseph, he was gone. Reuben was distraught. After selling Joseph, the other brothers took Joseph's coat and dipped it in a dead goat's blood and went home. **Genesis 37:32:** *"They took the ornate robe back to their father and said, 'We found this. Examine it to see whether it is your son's robe.'"* Jacob believed his son Joseph had been killed and devoured by an animal. For a long time he mourned for his son, refusing to be comforted. In the meantime, Joseph was sold again, this time to Potiphar, an officer of Pharaoh and captain of the guards. The story deviates to the consequences Judah suffered, and was told of before the continuation of the story of Joseph. A must-read is chapter 38 in the Book of Genesis. It is a forewarning that none of us are exempt from the consequences of our lies, not even Judah—the family line from which Jesus Christ descended.

---

Potiphar's Wife's Lie: The Lord was with Joseph and blessed him to prosper. He was promoted as overseer of the entire household of Potiphar, the Egyptian governor. Joseph was trustworthy, and Potiphar trusted Joseph with all that he had. God blessed the Egyptian's house for Joseph's sake. As time passed, Potiphar's wife started looking at Joseph with interest, and asked him to have her sexually. He refused to betray her husband; and he refused to betray God. Every day she continually begged Joseph to have sexual relations with her. One day when Joseph was about his business and no others were around, Potiphar's wife grabbed his clothing, insisting he have her. He ran away from her, leaving his garment behind. **Genesis 39:14-15:** *"She called her household servants. 'Look,' she said to them, 'this Hebrew has been brought to us to make sport of us! He came in here to sleep with me, but I screamed. When he heard me scream for help, he left his cloak beside me and ran out of the house.'"*

Potiphar's wife lied and accused Joseph of trying to rape her. She laid his garment next to her until her husband came home, then she lied to him. **Genesis 39:17-18:** *"Then she told him this story: 'That Hebrew slave you brought us came to me to make sport of me. But as soon as I screamed for help, he left his cloak beside me and ran out of the house.'"* Potiphar was fiercely angered. He put Joseph in the prison where the king's prisoners were bound. God was with Joseph even in prison, and He had the same favor with the prison warden as he had with Potiphar. He had even put Joseph in charge of the other prisoners, and made him his chief servant. Joseph would eventually be taken from prison by Pharaoh and put in charge of his home. Joseph was made second, only to Pharaoh, and he eventually made Joseph ruler of all Egypt.

---

Joseph's Lies: When all the land was experiencing a famine except Egypt, everyone went to Egypt to purchase food. Pharaoh appointed Joseph in charge of the food. Jacob, Joseph's father, sent his sons to Egypt to buy food, so they may live. When his sons saw Joseph, he was then unrecognizable, and he concealed his identity. His brothers bowed down to Joseph, just as he had prophesied in his youth. **Genesis 42:9:** *"Then he [Joseph] remembered his dreams about them and said to them, 'You are spies! You have come to see where our land is unprotected.'"* Joseph actually knew they were his brothers. The brothers explained who they were and told of their family, including their missing brother. **Genesis 42:14:** *"Joseph said to them, 'It is just as I told you: You are spies!'"*

Joseph said they would not go further unless one went to get their younger brother Benjamin. Joseph also said this was to prove they were not spies. Joseph set a scenario in order to send food back to his family and to learn of the truth regarding his departure from his family.

Joseph cried when he learned the truth. Joseph gave them plenty of food and unbeknown to them, returned the money they paid. The entire scenario left his brothers perplexed.

The brother's second visit to Joseph was to receive grain and return the money they presumed was mistakenly given back to them. Joseph devised a ploy to see his brother Benjamin-he falsely accused his other brothers. **Genesis 44:4-5:** *"They had not gone far from the city when Joseph said to his steward, 'Go after those men at once, and when you catch up with them, say to them, 'Why have you repaid good with evil? Isn't this the cup my master drinks from and also uses for divination? This is a wicked thing you have done.'"*

But this was not so; Joseph had his steward secretly place a silver cup in his brother's sack, then accused them of stealing it. The brothers rightfully refuted the accusations, and stated if anyone had the stolen cup, they would become Joseph's servant. The cup was found in Benjamin's sack, as Joseph had it placed there. Joseph then told the brothers he only wanted the man who had his cup-the rest may go home in peace to their father. The brothers fervently explained why it would devastate their father to near death if they did not return with their brother. Judah begged Joseph to make him a servant instead, and set Benjamin free to return to their father. He could not stand to see the state of their father if Benjamin was not returned.

Joseph finally reveals himself to his brothers! He then asks how his father is, and if he's still alive. His brothers were so troubled they were rendered speechless. Joseph asked them to come close to him and not to grieve or be angry at themselves, as God had placed him there to save their lives. He assured them it was not them who sent him to Egypt, but God. Also, that God had made him a ruler throughout the land. He asked them to bring his father, the entire family, and all they owned to be with him and survive the famine in prosperity. Everyone in Pharaoh's house was excited for Joseph and his family, and Pharaoh offered all the good of the land to them.

Jacob, whose name was changed to Israel by God, was excited to see his son again before dying.

---

All the generations of Jacob left for Goshen, every man, woman, and child. When Joseph saw his father, he hugged his neck and cried for a great while. Jacob, called Israel, was so elated he said he could now die, as he has seen his son alive. It was proper for Joseph to present his family to Pharaoh. The men were shepherds by trade. Joseph instructed them to lie when Pharaoh asked their occupation. **Genesis 46:34** *"You should answer, 'Your servants have tended livestock from our boyhood on, just as our fathers did.' Then you will be allowed to settle in the region of Goshen, for all shepherds are detestable to the Egyptians."*

Joseph presented five of his brothers to Pharaoh, who asked them their occupation. They told the truth. They said they were shepherds, and so were their previous generations. They also said more, explaining that their purpose for coming to the new land was because their land lacked pasture for their flocks due to the famine. The truth proved superior. Pharaoh told Joseph to put his brothers and father in the best of the land. Joseph presented his father to Pharaoh. Jacob blessed Pharaoh and left his presence. Joseph's family was given possession of land in Egypt, the land of Rameses, as Pharaoh commanded. In that land their possessions multiplied exceedingly.

---

Jacob prophesied and blessed his twelve sons accordingly: Reuben, Simeon, Levi, Judah, Issachar, Dan, Gad, Asher, Naphtali, Joseph, and Benjamin; the twelve tribes of Israel. He prophesied what would be the future consequences of the choices they made in life. Afterward, he went to bed and died. Joseph fell on his father's face and cried and kissed him. He then honored his father's wish to be buried in the land of Canaan.

After the period of mourning and burial, they returned to Egypt. Now that their father was dead, Joseph's brothers feared he would hate them and make them pay for what they had done to him in the past. They lied to Joseph, using their dead father to curtail any vengeance from Joseph. **Genesis 50:16-17:** *"So they sent word to Joseph, saying, 'Your father left these instructions before he died: "This is what you are to say to Joseph: I ask you to forgive your brothers the sins and the wrongs they committed in treating you so badly." Now please forgive the sins of the servants of the God of your father.' When their message came to him, Joseph wept."* His brothers bowed before him and offered to be his servants. Joseph told them to not fear him; for vengeance is God's, not his. God allowed it all to happen to save many lives. He told them what they meant for evil, God meant it for good. Joseph had long forgiven his brothers. He spoke kindly to them and assured them they were forgiven.

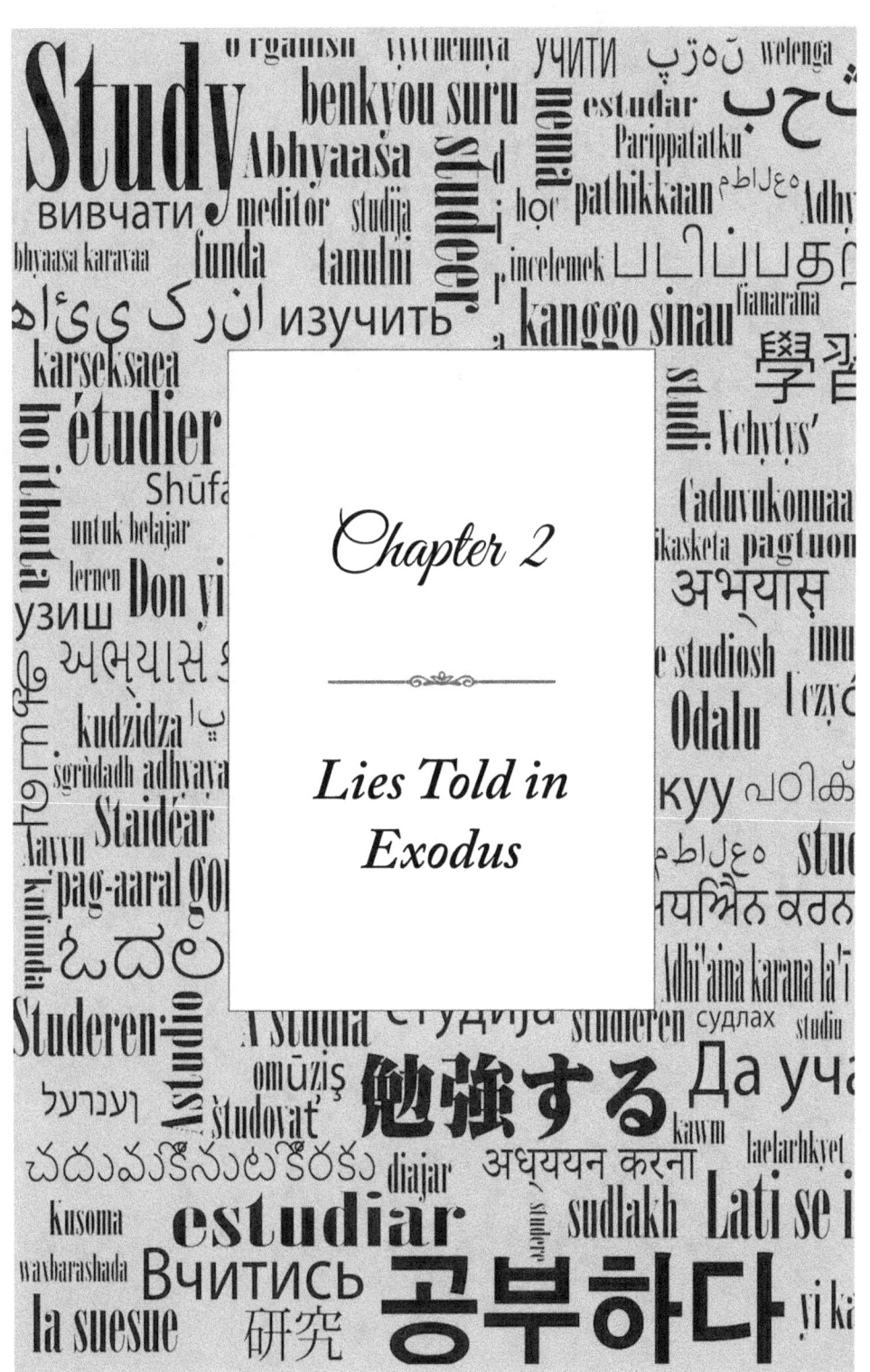

# Chapter 2

## Lies Told in Exodus

Midwives' Lie: Time passed on and Joseph and all his generation had passed on as well. The Israelites grew numerous; and Egypt grew, filled with them. A new Pharaoh arose who knew nothing about Joseph. This king thought the Israelites were too numerous; if a war started they could join the enemy, fighting against Egypt. He placed slave masters over them and forced them into slave labor. The Israelites built great cities for this Pharaoh.

The more they were afflicted, the more they multiplied in number. The king of Egypt told the midwives to kill all baby boys delivered by Hebrew women. Female infants could live. The midwives feared God and kept the newborn boys alive. The king asked them why they disobeyed him and saved the male babies. **Exodus 1:19: *"The midwives answered Pharaoh, 'Hebrew women are not like Egyptian women; they are vigorous and give birth before the midwives arrive.'"*** The midwives lied, stating the babies were birthed before they could get to the mothers! God dealt well with those midwives; because they feared God, He blessed them with houses and their own children. The Israelites continued to multiply. Then Pharaoh ordered all of his people to throw the Hebrew boys into the river to drown (Exodus 1:22).

---

Pharaoh's Lies: Moses continually went to Pharaoh to tell him that God said, "Let my people go, that they may serve Me." Pharaoh refused. The Lord had hardened Pharaoh's heart. He told Moses so. The plague of frogs covered over all the land. Frogs were in people's beds, ovens, everywhere. Pharaoh then said he would let God's people go so they could offer sacrifices to the Lord. **Exodus 8:8: *"Pharaoh summoned Moses and Aaron and said, 'Pray to the Lord to take the frogs away from me and my people, and I will let your people go to offer sacrifices to the Lord.'"*** Moses responded that tomorrow he would, so that Pharaoh would surely know there is no other like the Lord our God. Moses asked God to remove the frogs, which then all died. The dead frogs were gathered up in heaps and the land stank. When Pharaoh got relief from the frogs, he hardened his heart and did not let God's people go. Because Pharaoh did not honor his word, it was rendered a lie.

Then God told Moses to tell Aaron to use the rod to cover all of Egypt with lice and then flies. God put a division between those who served Him and the others. In the land of Goshen where God's people were, there were no flies. This was a sure sign the swarms were the work of God. The land of Egypt was ruined because of the swarm of flies. **Exodus 8:28:** *"Pharaoh said, 'I will let you go to offer sacrifices to the Lord your God in the wilderness, but you must not go very far. Now pray for me.'"* Pharaoh "fixed" the lie oh so well, sounding so convincing; even asking Moses to petition, to pray, for him. Habitual liars lie to a science; the same science typical of live dynamite. Destruction is imminent. The Lord did what Moses asked and removed swarms of flies from Pharaoh. Not one fly remained. But once again, Pharaoh dealt deceitfully with Moses, hardened his heart, and would not let the people go.

God raised up Pharaoh and allowed all this to occur to show to their unbelief His power—that the name of the Lord God would be declared throughout all the earth. God then spoke that He would cause it to rain hail more grievous than ever before or ever will be. Any human or animal it fell upon, it killed. There were also some Egyptians who feared God and believed the Word of God and kept their animals and people inside. Those who did not fear or believe left their people and animals in the field. God struck with hail and fire mingled with the hail. Every field and its contents were destroyed (Exodus 9:23-25). Only in the land of Goshen, where the children of Israel were, no hail fell.

**Exodus 9:27:** *"Then Pharaoh summoned Moses and Aaron. 'This time I have sinned,' he said to them. 'The Lord is in the right, and I and my people are in the wrong.'"* Pharaoh was lying, saying what he thought

Moses would want to hear; calculating words to persuade Moses to stop the hail. When Pharaoh said he would let the people go, Moses knew he was lying. Moses stopped the hail so that Pharaoh would know the earth is the Lord's and God is able. Once again, Pharaoh hardened his heart and did not let the people go; just as God had spoken to Moses. God allowed these signs and many others so from generation to generation we would tell of these signs and know that He is God.

God allowed Moses and the people of Israel to leave Egypt after the Passover observance. By then, the Egyptians were anxious for them to leave. The people of Israel took all they owned and began their journey. God brought them out of the land of Egypt, through the wilderness toward a land with great promises (Exodus 12:31-51).

God hardened Pharaoh's heart again and Pharaoh went after the children of Israel with his army. As Pharaoh's army approached, some of the people became fearful and cried out to the Lord. Some asked Moses why they would now die in the wilderness, when none had died in Egypt. They asked why he led them out of Egypt. How soon they had forgotten their many years of hardships in Egypt. They continued to complain.

The People of Israel's Lies: **Exodus 14:12:** *"Didn't we say to you in Egypt, 'Leave us alone; let us serve the Egyptians'? It would have been better for us to serve the Egyptians than to die in the desert!"* Their words were not true. Yes, the words were said in fear of their lives, but they were not true. Moses told the people to fear not, stand still, and see the salvation of the Lord. God would rid them of Pharaoh and his army forever. Moses said for the people to hold their peace, God would fight for them. As they approached the sea, the Lord told Moses to stretch out his hand over the sea. God then divided the sea with a strong wind and allowed them to escape the army of Pharaoh on dry land, between two walls of water. After they were safe, the waters fell down over the Egyptians in pursuit of the children of Israel, and they all drowned. Not one survived. The Lord saved Israel that day (Genesis 14:21-31). All of Israel saw the mighty work of the Lord, and feared and believed the Lord and His servant Moses.

The people sang and honored God for their triumph, but their gratitude was short-lived. As soon as their physical needs weren't being met, they started murmuring and complaining. How soon we all forget. Like ungrateful children—and no one appreciates ungrateful children. We need to simply remember the goodness that God has just done for us, and trust in God to bring us through to the next triumph. God clearly allows situations to occur so we can "remember" that it is He who brings us through them. These stories are faith-building; for *"without faith it is impossible to please God"* (Hebrews 11:6).

Unfortunately, the children of Israel continued to complain against Moses and Aaron. **Exodus 16:3:** ***"The Israelites said to them, 'If only we had died by the Lord's hand in Egypt! There we sat around pots of meat and ate all the food we wanted, but you have brought us out into this desert to starve this entire assembly to death.'"*** This was an untruthful, malicious, and spiteful exaggeration. When something said is not the truth, what is it? A lie! Be cautious of gross exaggerations with ill-gotten motives; they become seared in minds.

The Lord God miraculously provided food and water for the children of Israel—right there in the wilderness. God didn't take them out of the wilderness at that time; rather, He provided for them in their current circumstance. And God provided in ways so that they would surely know the provision was from Him.

God the Father always wants His children to acknowledge Him and to thank Him. God told Moses to establish the Sabbath statutes as a covenant forever. At that time, God had Moses depart from the people and go into His presence. The people thought Moses' departure lasted too long, so they asked Aaron to make them a god, which he did, out of gold—a golden calf. **Exodus 32:4:** ***"He took what they handed him and made it into an idol cast in the shape of a calf, fashioning it with a tool. Then they said, 'These are your gods, Israel,*** *who brought you up out of Egypt.'"* The people lied and credited a cow (which they crafted with gold from their own jewelry) with praise for their freedom from Egypt. It was pure rebellion—God had commanded them not to have any other gods before Him. When God delivers, of a certainty, only God gets the credit. We are in error when we have idols, items, or images as necessary points of contact for worship.

Then Aaron lied to Moses regarding how the calf came to exist. **Exodus 32:24:** *"So I told them, 'Whoever has any gold jewelry, take it off.' Then they gave me the gold, and I threw it into the fire, and out came this calf!"* Partial truth equates to a lie. Telling half-truths make a liar and a deceiver. Therefore, the Lord plagued the people. The Word of God— the Bible—makes it clear that Aaron made the calf.

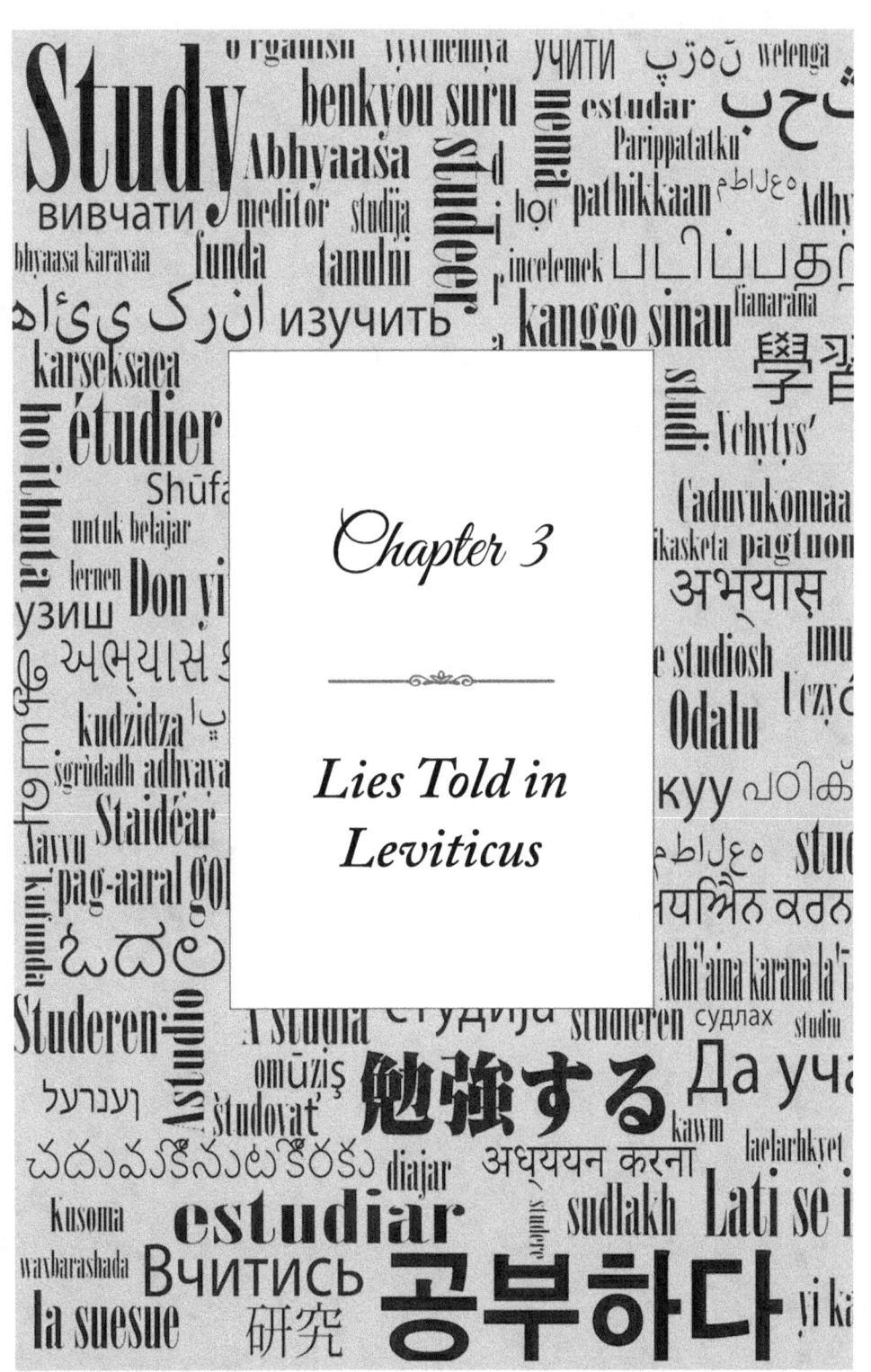

*Chapter 3*

*Lies Told in Leviticus*

As I began to read the Book of Leviticus, the Holy Spirit revealed to me that there were no lies told here, but I was to include instructions for us concerning telling lies, as taught in Leviticus. No one lied, but God has a Word against lying. In the Book of Leviticus, the Lord told Moses that if someone lies to or deceives his or her neighbor, that person must restore what the neighbor (any person) lost due to the lie, or whatever was gained in the deception. This is part of a person's forgiveness. Forgiveness for lying comes with required action. Also, if you find a lost item, it is a sin if you lie concerning it. In Leviticus, God clearly states that we should not lie to one another.

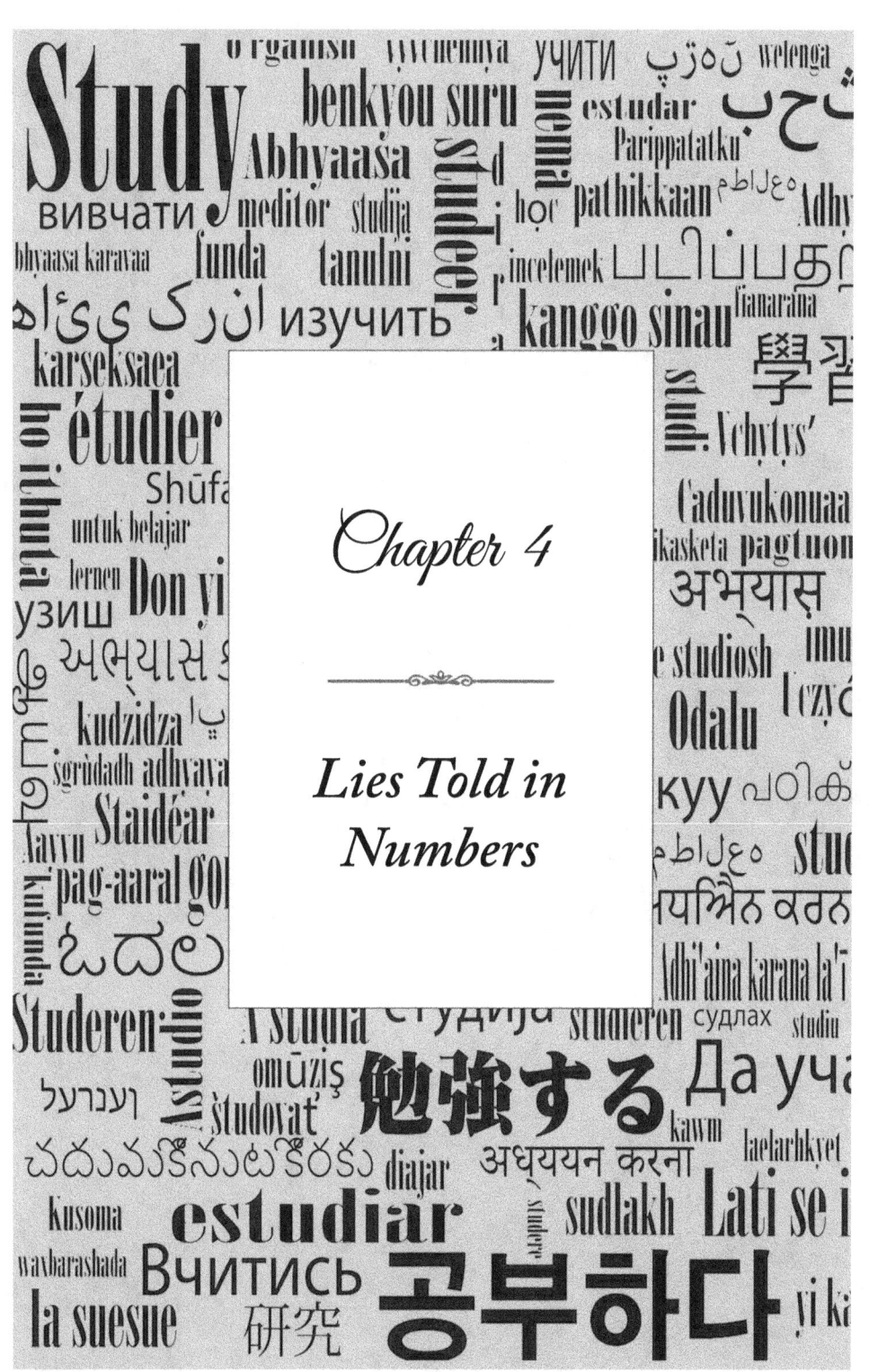

# Chapter 4

## Lies Told in Numbers

The Children of Israel's Lies: The children of Israel were in the wilderness on their journey to the land promised to them by God. When it was reported that there were giants in that land, the people were fearful and complained, doubting God. **Numbers 14:3:** *"Why is the Lord bringing us to this land only to let us fall by the sword? Our wives and children will be taken as plunder. Wouldn't it be better for us to go back to Egypt?"* In this manner of questioning God, they spoke lying accusations against God. Their sin was not in questioning God, but lying. God later let them know that they themselves would not see the Promised Land, but one day their children, whom they accused God of turning into prey, would.

*Their sin was not in questioning God, but lying.*

The people blamed Moses for all they encountered in the wilderness. Moses assured them that all he had instructed the people to do was from God's guidance. He had done nothing of his own mind. God performed a new thing in the earth and took out the sinful complainers. It was powerfully evident it was God's doing—not Moses or Aaron, or any other person. The people saw the mighty act of God and feared God, lest God took them out likewise. **Numbers 16:41:** *"The next day the whole Israelite community grumbled against Moses and Aaron. 'You have killed the Lord's people,' they said."* They had witnessed a powerful act of God, and the very next day they told lies, accusing Moses and Aaron. Even so, Moses and Aaron tried frantically to atone for the sins of those whose lying accusations were against them. God killed those liars anyway (Numbers 16:49).

# Chapter 5

## Lies Told in Joshua

Rahab's Lie: The prostitute Rahab hid the spies sent by Joshua in an effort to help them. The two spies lodged at her home because they were being sought after by the king's men. **Joshua 2:4-5**: *"But the woman had taken the two men and hidden them. She said, 'Yes, the men came to see me, but I did not know where they had come from.'"* At dusk, when it was time to close the city gate, they left. *"I don't know which way they went. Go after them quickly. You may catch up with them."* Rahab lied about the men's whereabouts to save their lives.

Once the danger was averted, she told the two men she was aware that they were Israelites; and she was aware of their history and of God's deliverance of their people. She also said she was aware of how God had divided the Red Sea for the Israelites. She continued, saying she knew their God was the true God of heaven and earth, and that God had given that land to the Israelites. The two men promised her she would be spared, along with all in her household, if she continued to help them, telling no one of their plans. She honored her word, and the men honored their word; and they all lived (Joshua 2:14). When the Israelites took the land of Jericho, Joshua instructed the two spies to save Rahab the harlot and her household from death, just as they had sworn they would.

---

The Hivites' Lies: All the lands near and far heard how Joshua and the Israelites took the land they knew God had promised them. The people from the land of Gibeon (called Hivites) devised a scheme of lies, supposedly to spare their lives from being taken when their land was to be pursued. **Joshua 9:6**: *"Then they went to Joshua in the camp at Gilgal and said to him and the Israelites, 'We have come from a distant country; make a treaty with us.'"* The Hivites told Joshua they came to become servants. **Joshua 9:12-13**: *"This bread of ours was warm when we packed it at home on the day we left to come to* *you. But now see how dry and moldy it is. And these wineskins that we filled were new, but see how cracked they are. And our clothes and sandals are worn out by the very long journey,"* Actually they were from a nearby town, yet lied to appear to have traveled from a timely and far distance.

Because the Israelites did not seek the counsel of the Lord, they swore an oath with the Hivites. Three days later they learned the truth of the Hivites having come from the land close by. The Israelites honored the oath they swore with the Hivites, and let them live; but, they were cursed for the lies they told. The Israelites knew if they did not honor their word, the wrath of God would be upon them. The Hivites were cursed to remain servants, which was acceptable to them, as they were allowed to live. The Hivites received the ramifications of their lies, as we all do. They did not have evil intentions, so their lives were spared. They were cursed because, as with all lies, there is an equitable cost.

# Chapter 6

## Lies Told in Judges

Abimelek's Lie: Abimelek is lying in the form of a deceptive question. **Judges 9:2:** *"Ask all the citizens of Shechem, 'Which is better for you: to have all seventy of Jerub-Baal's sons rule over you, or just that one man?' Remember, I am your flesh and blood."* A lie spoken entangled in a question is still a lie. Prevarication in any form—someone deliberately deviating from the truth—is lying. The wickedness that occurred as Abimelek continued his deceitful acts ensued. Abimelek was

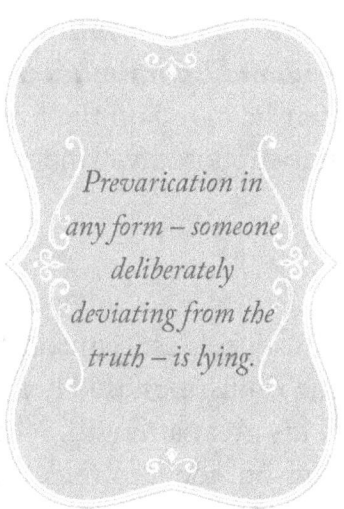

*Prevarication in any form – someone deliberately deviating from the truth – is lying.*

also a murderer. God sent an evil spirit to deal with Abimelek. Wickedness begets, or births, wickedness. In God's doing, Abimelek was killed by a woman. But so large was Abimelek's pride, that he had his armor bearer thrust his sword through him so it wouldn't be known that a woman killed him—yet we are acknowledging it still today (Judges 9:54).

---

The Ephraimites' Lies: Jephthah, who lead Israel for six years, led the men of Gilead to fight and kill the Ephraimites because they told lies about the Gileadites. **Judges 12:4:** *"Jephthah then called together the men of Gilead and fought against Ephraim. The Gileadites struck them down because the Ephraimites had said, 'You Gileadites are renegades from Ephraim and Manasseh.'"* The Gileadites continued to physically catch the escaped Ephraimites by "catching" them in their lie regarding who they really were.

**Judges 12:5-6:** *"The Gileadites captured the fords of the Jordan leading to Ephraim, and whenever a survivor of Ephraim said, 'Let me cross over,' the men of Gilead asked him, 'Are you an Ephraimite?' If he replied, 'No,' they said, 'All right, say "Shibboleth."' If he said, 'Sibboleth,' because he could not pronounce the word correctly, they* *seized him and killed him at the fords of the Jordan. Forty-two thousand Ephraimites were killed at that time."* They were caught in their lie based on their inability to pronounce the name of the place they supposedly came from!

---

Samson's Lies: Samson fell in love with a woman named Delilah. The Philistines used her to entice Samson into telling her the source of his great strength. Not only was she aware they wanted to afflict Samson, she also took an offer of money to assist them. She asked Samson the source of his strength and how he might be bound. **Judges 16:7:** *"Samson answered her, 'If anyone ties me with seven fresh bowstrings that have not been dried, I'll become as weak as any other man.'"* Samson lied. Delilah tried to bind him as he said, and he easily broke free. She had the Philistine men hiding in her room to harm Samson. She continued her ploy, accused him of lying, and pleaded with him to learn of his strength. **Judges 16:11:** *"He said, 'If anyone ties me securely with new ropes that have never been used, I'll become as weak as any other man.'"* This was another similar scenario with similar results. Samson broke the ropes like they were thread. Samson had lied to her again.

And once more, Samson lied to her. **Judges 16:13:** *"Delilah then said to Samson, 'All this time you have been making a fool of me and lying to me. Tell me how you can be tied.' He replied, 'If you weave the seven braids of my head into the fabric on the loom and tighten it with the pin, I'll become as weak as any other man.' So while he was sleeping, Delilah took the seven braids of his head [and] wove them into the fabric."* Her attempt to bind him again did not work. Delilah cried out to Samson saying that he could not possibly love her, mocking her those three times. She pressed and urged Samson daily, so much so it wore on him to his core unbearably. Samson eventually told Delilah the truth of his strength. She should not have been made privy to that information, and she used it wickedly against Samson.

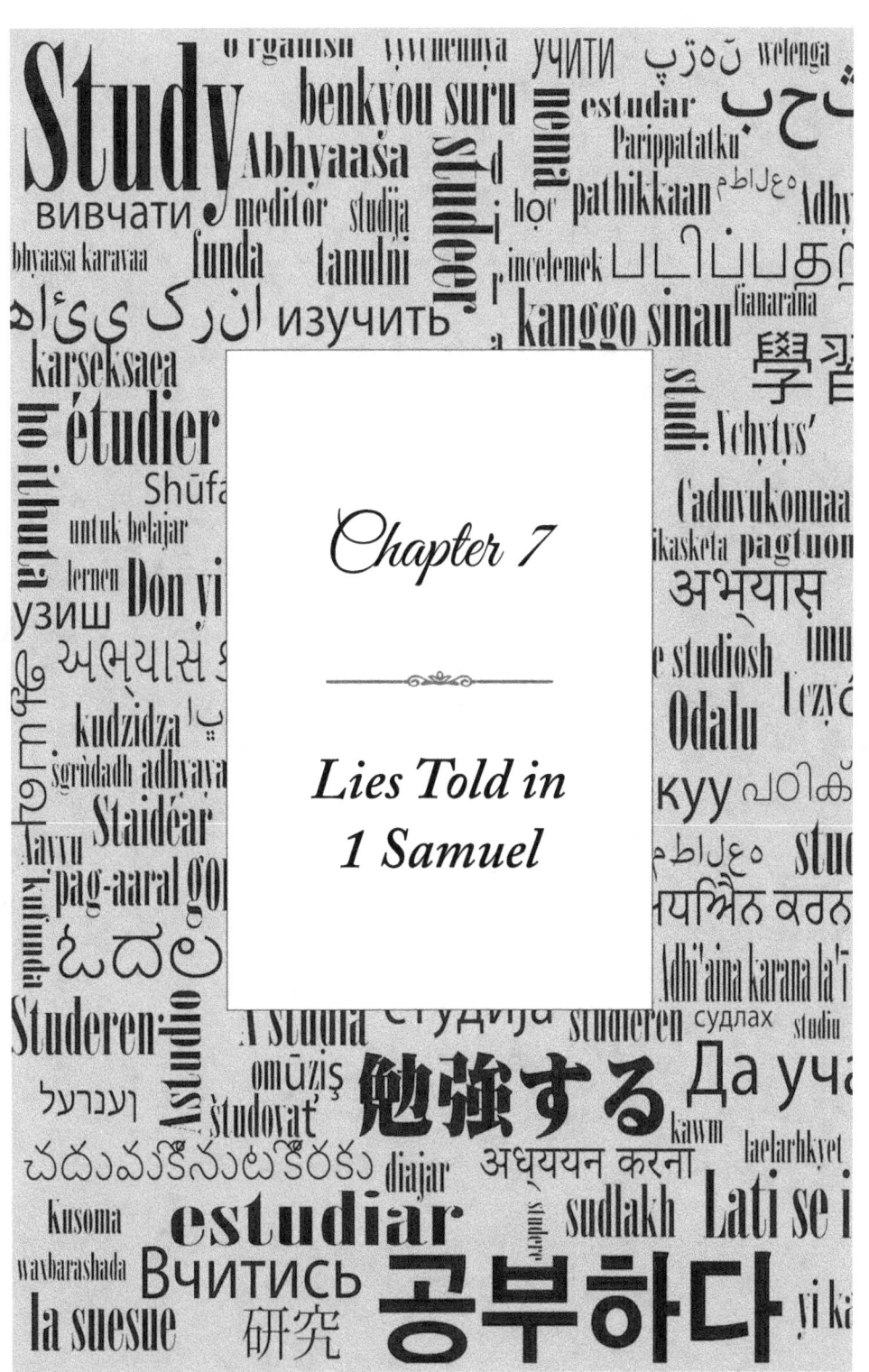

# Chapter 7

## Lies Told in 1 Samuel

Saul's Lies: Saul, the first king appointed over the Israelites called for the people to observe a fast; but his son Jonathan ate some honey in defiance. Jonathan truthfully told his father what he had done. **1 Samuel 14:44:** *"Saul said, 'May God deal with me, be it ever so severely, if you do not die, Jonathan.'"* The people rescued Jonathan as he had just rescued them in a mighty way against the Philistines. They refused to let anything happen to Jonathan and he did not die. Saul had spoken that it was God's doing that Jonathan should die. Apparently it wasn't so.

Eliab's Lie: David's father sent him to take food to his older brothers as they fought against the Philistines. Goliath the giant had already challenged the Israelites, and Saul and his army were afraid. David inquired of the circumstances of this giant who challenged the army of God. **1 Samuel 17:28:** *"When Eliab, David's oldest brother, heard him speaking with the men, he burned with anger at him and asked, 'Why have you come down here? And with whom did you leave those few sheep in the wilderness? I know how conceited you are and how wicked your heart is; you came down only to watch the battle.'"* David's older brother lied about his purpose for being there. And he made verbal attempts to discourage David.

Many great accomplishments in history would have been obliterated if the individuals had accepted discouraging words of naysayers and liars. David did not let his big brother's words define him. Sometimes others' discouraging words can come from their own jealousy and guilt. David had really done nothing to warrant his brother's anger toward him. David aligned his abilities with the power of God and killed Goliath. David believed the words of God, not man.

Saul had promised that the one who slayed Goliath would wed his daughter. **1 Samuel 18:17:** *"Saul said to David, 'Here is my older daughter Merab. I will give her to you in marriage; only serve me bravely and fight the battles of the Lord.' For Saul said to himself, 'I will not raise a hand against him. Let the Philistines do that!'"* Yet when it was time for David to marry Merab, Saul's daughter, Saul gave her to another man in marriage. Saul secretly wanted David to be killed in battle by the Philistines, so he wouldn't have to kill David himself.

Saul's other daughter fell in love with David, but David said he was too poor to wed a king's daughter; as he had no dowry to give. The servants reported David's concern to Saul. **1 Samuel 18:25:** *"Saul replied, 'Say to David, "The king wants no other price for the bride than a hundred Philistine foreskins, to take revenge on his enemies."' Saul's plan was to have David fall by the hands of the Philistines."* Saul lied in hopes of a perfect plot to have David killed. David triumphed, which made Saul more afraid of David. Saul envied David even more as he saw that God was with David; also, his daughter loved David.

---

Jonathan's Lie: Jonathan lied to King Saul, his father, to save the life of David; his friend that he loved as much as himself. **1 Samuel 20:28-29:** *"Jonathan answered, 'David earnestly asked me for permission to go to Bethlehem. He said, "Let me go, because our family is observing a sacrifice in the town and my brother has ordered me to be there. If I have found favor in your eyes, let me get away to see my brothers." That is why he has not come to the king's table.'"* This was part of David and Jonathan's scheme to keep David away from Saul, who wanted to kill David.

---

David's Lies: In hiding from Saul, David lied to Ahimelek the priest. **1 Samuel 21:2:** *"David answered Ahimelek the priest, 'The king sent me on a mission and said to me, "No one is to know anything about the mission I am sending you on." As for my men, I have told them to meet me at a certain place.'"* Telling a lie is David's first biblically noted sin. David felt compelled to continue lying. **1 Samuel 21:8:** *"David asked Ahimelek, 'Don't you have a spear or a sword here? I haven't brought my sword or any other weapon, because the king's mission was urgent.'"*

# Chapter 8

## Lies Told in 2 Samuel

A Young Man's Lie: Three days after the death of Saul, a young man came to David as one mourning. He told David, "Saul was dead." **2 Samuel 1:3:** *"'Where have you come from?' David asked him. He answered, 'I have escaped from the Israelite camp.'"* David asked the man how he knew Saul and his son Jonathan were dead. **2 Samuel 1:6-10:** *"'I happened to be on Mount Gilboa,' the young man said, 'and there was Saul, leaning on his spear, with the chariots and their drivers in hot pursuit. When he turned around and saw me, he called out to me, and I said, "What can I do?" He asked me, "Who are you?" "An Amalekite," I answered.*

*Then he said to me, "Stand here by me and kill me! I'm in the throes of death, but I'm still alive." So I stood beside him and killed him, because I knew that after he had fallen he could not survive. And I took the crown that was on his head and the band on his arm and have brought them here to my lord.'"*

The young man had lied and fabricated the entire story in hopes of gaining from David. It was widely known that Saul desired to take David's life. Yet David did not rejoice over Saul's death, he mourned and cried instead. Then he had that man killed for having the audacity to kill Saul, God's anointed. What had appeared to be a perfect scheme of lies cost the man his life.

David's Lies: David fell in love with Bathsheba's beauty and had sexual relations with her, although he knew she was married to his warrior Uriah. She became pregnant by David who brought Uriah out from battle to go home to have sexual relations with his wife Bathsheba. Uriah was an honorable man and would not go to the comforts of home and his wife while the other men were in the battlefields. So then David had Uriah strategically placed on the front line of the battle, making his death certain. David had Uriah killed. **2 Samuel 11:25:** *"David told the messenger, 'Say this to Joab: "Don't let this upset you; the sword devours one as well as another. Press the attack against the city and destroy it." Say this to encourage Joab.'"* This lie was spoken as a cover-up. David was trying to minimize Uriah's death as just another death in war, just as others who had died. This displeased God, and David paid extensively for all he had done.

---

David's Nephew's Lie: David's son Amnon raped his own half-sister Tamar. She was very beautiful and he fell sickly in love with her. After he raped her, he immediately hated her with the same intensity. Her brother Absalom and Absalom's father, David, were deeply angered; but several years passed and nothing was done to Amnon. Then Absalom received permission for all of David's sons—Absalom's brothers—to journey with him to a place near Ephraim. At this time he had Amnon killed. Everyone then scattered. **2 Samuel 13:30:** *"While they were on their way, the report came to David: 'Absalom has struck down all the king's sons; not one of them is left.'"* In grief and anguish, David fell to the ground tearing his clothing, believing all his sons were dead. Then David's nephew assured him only Amnon was dead. Absalom had planned to kill Amnon from the very day he raped his sister. David was comforted knowing not all of his sons were dead. He was also comforted regarding Amnon's death.

---

An Older Woman's Lie: Joab, David's military leader, devised a plan to have Absalom returned home to his father. He had an older woman lie, pretending to be a widower, a long time in mourning. Joab put words in her mouth to say to King David. **2 Samuel 14:4-7:** *"When the woman from Tekoa went to the king, she fell with her face to the ground to pay him honor, and she said, 'Help me, Your Majesty!' The king asked her, 'What is troubling you?' She said, 'I am a widow; my husband is dead. I your servant had two sons. They got into a fight with each other in the field, and no one was there to separate them. One struck the other and killed him. Now the whole clan has risen up against your servant; they say, "Hand over the one who struck his brother down, so that we may put him to death for the life of his brother whom he killed; then we will get rid of the heir as well." They would put out the only burning coal I have left, leaving my husband neither name nor descendant on the face of the earth.'"*

The lies spoken were an attempt to have David notice the correlation to his situation with Absalom. David asked her if Joab was the one who sent her, and told her what to say. David, in his wisdom from God, knew and understood Joab's determination. Joab had no wicked intentions, and David honored his request to have Absalom returned unharmed.

---

Absalom's Lie: After time had passed, Absalom started going early to King David's gate and redirected anyone coming to the king for justice in lawsuits and controversial states of affairs. **2 Samuel 15:3:** *"Then Absalom would say to him, 'Look, your claims are valid and proper, but there is no representative of the king to hear you.'"* Absalom lied to take control of the government himself. It was part of his long-term plan to win the hearts of the people. He conspired to become king. And he did, after forty years of coercion and deception. David, though still king himself, ran and hid from Absalom, his own son.

---

Ziba's Lie: As David was fleeing Absalom, he met Ziba, Mephibosheth's servant, in the mountains. Ziba brought numerous gifts of food, animals, and wine for David and his men. **2 Samuel 16:3:** *"The king then asked, 'Where is your master's grandson?' Ziba said to him, 'He is staying in Jerusalem, because he thinks, "Today the Israelites will restore to me my grandfather's kingdom."'"* Ziba was lying about Mephibosheth in the heinous act of taking advantage of someone because of his physical disabilities. David believed Ziba's lie and awarded him everything that belonged to Mephibosheth.

---

Hushai's Lie: David's friend, Hushai, left to join Absalom, pretending to serve Absalom so he could report back to David whatever was being said by Absalom. Absalom asked Hushai why he didn't join his friend David and support him. **2 Samuel 16:18:** *"Hushai said to Absalom, 'No, the one chosen by the Lord, by these people, and by all the men of Israel—his I will be, and I will remain with him.'"* Hushai was lying in order to help David. **2 Samuel 16:19:** *"Furthermore, whom should I serve? Should I not serve the son? Just as I served your father, so I will serve you."* Then again Hushai lied to Absalom, insinuating killing David and his men. **2 Samuel 17:12:** *"Then we will attack him wherever he may be found, and we will fall on him as dew settles on the ground. Neither he nor any of his men will be left alive."*

---

A Woman's Lie: A young boy told Absalom he saw David's men. A woman hid the two men in a covered well. **2 Samuel 17:20:** *"When Absalom's men came to the woman at the house, they asked, 'Where are*

*Ahimaaz and Jonathan?' The woman answered them, 'They crossed over the brook.' The men searched but found no one, so they returned to Jerusalem."* Yes, this woman also lied regarding the whereabouts of the two men to help them.

---

Ahimaaz's Lie: After Absalom died, Ahimaaz feared telling King David such news. **2 Samuel 18:29:** *"The king asked, 'Is the young man Absalom safe?' Ahimaaz answered, 'I saw great confusion just as Joab was about to send the king's servant and me, your servant, but I don't know what it was.'"* He lied because he could not bring himself to tell David the bad news of his son's death.

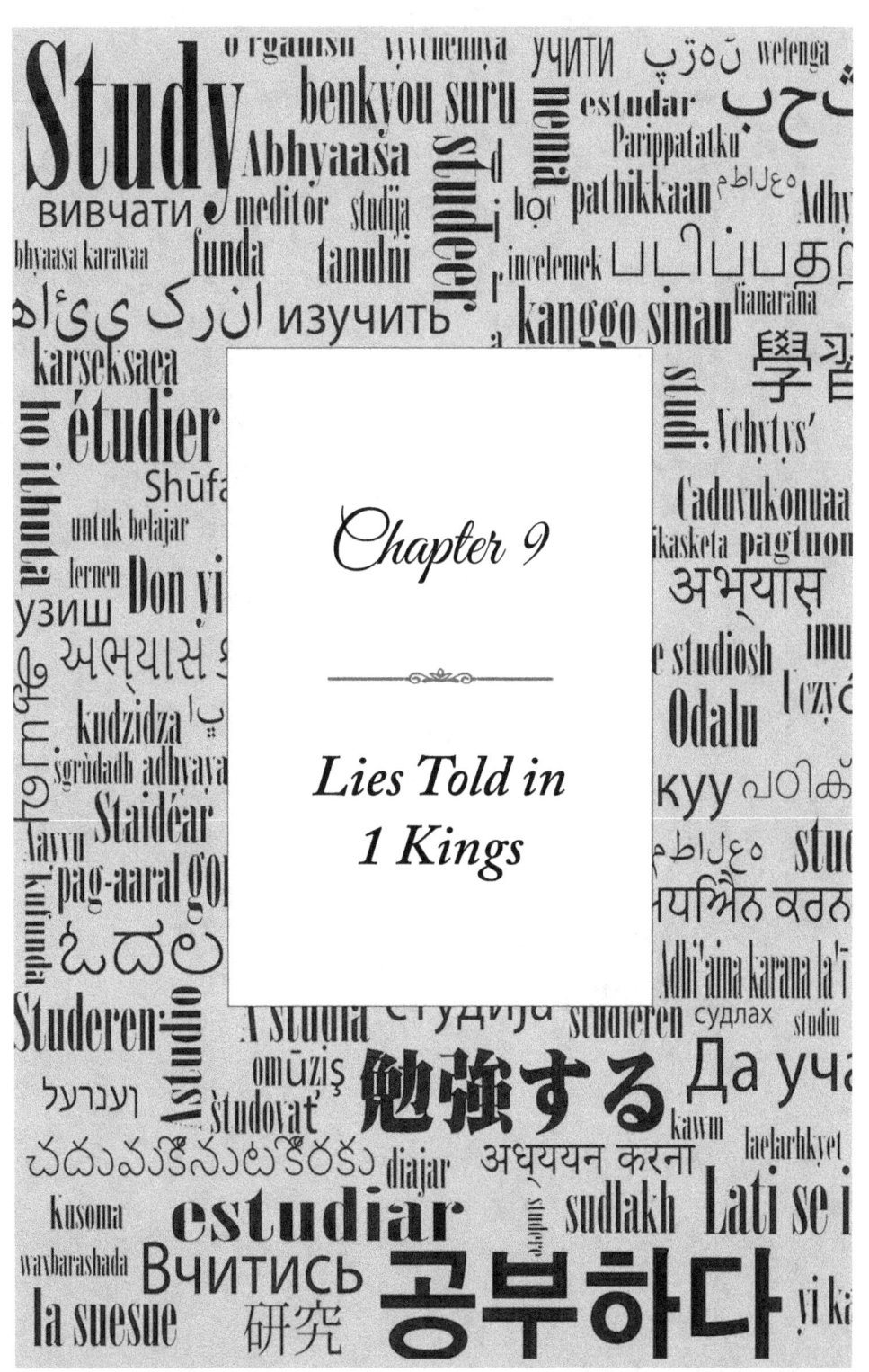

# Chapter 9

## Lies Told in 1 Kings

Dead Baby's Mother's Lie: Solomon was given untold wisdom from God to discern judgment. Two women, who lived together, both mothers of newborns, came to Solomon asking for judgment. One accused the other of waking in the night and switching their babies. One of their babies had died during the night. The woman speaking claimed the other had rolled over on her baby and mistakenly smothered the child. There were no witnesses to say which baby belonged to whom. **1 Kings 3:22: *"The other woman said, 'No! The living one is my son; the dead one is yours.' But the first one insisted, 'No! The dead one is yours; the living one is mine.' And so they argued before the king."***

King Solomon repeated their contention back to them. And then he asked his men to bring him a sword. **1 Kings 3:25: *"He then gave an order: 'Cut the living child in two and give half to one and half to the other.'"*** Then the true mother of the child cried out to give the child to the other woman. Under no circumstances did she want her child harmed. Yet, the other woman said let neither of us have the child, and agreed to divide the child. Then the king said to give the child to the rightful mother. Surely no one would kill the child—the obvious mother was now known.

---

The Old Prophet's Lie: A prophet spoke to King Jeroboam as God instructed. All that the prophet said would happen occurred. The king asked the prophet to go home with him and eat. The prophet said he was instructed of God to neither eat nor drink with him in that place, so the prophet continued on his journey. The sons of an old prophet in Bethel told their father of the other prophet, and the words from God he had spoken to the king. The old prophet extended the same invitation to the prophet to eat and drink. **1 Kings 13:18: *"The old prophet answered, 'I too am a prophet, as you are. And an***

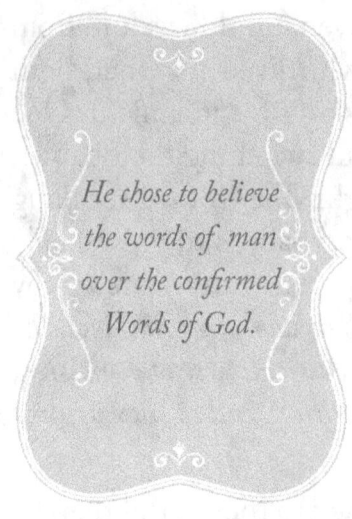

*He chose to believe the words of man over the confirmed Words of God.*

angel said to me by the word of the Lord: "Bring him back with you to your house so that he may eat bread and drink water."' (But he was lying to him.)"

The man of God believed the lies of the old prophet, and afterward he ate and drank with him. God spoke through the old prophet that the other prophet would die due to his disobedience to God's instructions. He chose to believe the words of man over the confirmed words of God. The prophet was soon killed by a lion, but the lion did not eat his body. The old prophet who lied, sorrowfully had the man's body placed in the grave he owned for himself. He requested of his sons that he be buried with the prophet when he dies.

---

Two Wicked Men's Lie: Jezebel, the wife of King Ahab, used two evil men in a plot to kill Naboth for his land adjacent to the king's palace. Naboth would not sell it to the king because he inherited the land from his father. When Jezebel saw how sad the king was about his inability to purchase Naboth's land, she told him to eat, drink, and be merry for she would get him the land. She made wicked men lie about Naboth to have him killed. **1 Kings 21:13:** *"Then two scoundrels came and sat opposite him and brought charges against Naboth before the people, saying, 'Naboth has cursed both God and the king.' So they took him outside the city and stoned him to death."* God spoke of the approaching death of Jezebel for her wicked ways. King Ahab earnestly humbled himself before God and God forgave him. Yet, a price had to be paid for his sins.

Micaiah's Lie: God actually led the prophets to prophesy falsely so the death of Ahab would occur. Three years had passed and King Ahab had remained in sin against God, provoking the people in sin also. **1 Kings 22:12:** *"All the other prophets were prophesying the same thing. 'Attack Ramoth Gilead and be victorious,' they said, 'for the Lord will give it into the king's hand.'"* King Jehoshaphat's chosen prophet, Micaiah, was called upon by a messenger who instructed him to prophesy something good. King Ahab had previously stated that this prophet never prophesied anything good to him. **1 Kings 22:15:** *"When he arrived, the king asked him, 'Micaiah, shall we go to war against Ramoth Gilead, or not?' 'Attack and be victorious,' he answered, 'for the Lord will give it into the king's hand.'"* He then told the truth when Jehoshaphat asked him how many times he has to tell him to not lie to him, but speak what is true in the name of the Lord. Then he prophesied the truth, which was that he saw Israel's people scattered without a leader. Micaiah the prophet said to Ahab, "If you return at all, the Lord has not spoken to me." Although King Ahab went to battle fully disguised, and his men were told their sole purpose was the safety of Ahab, he was still stabbed. King Ahab bled and died.

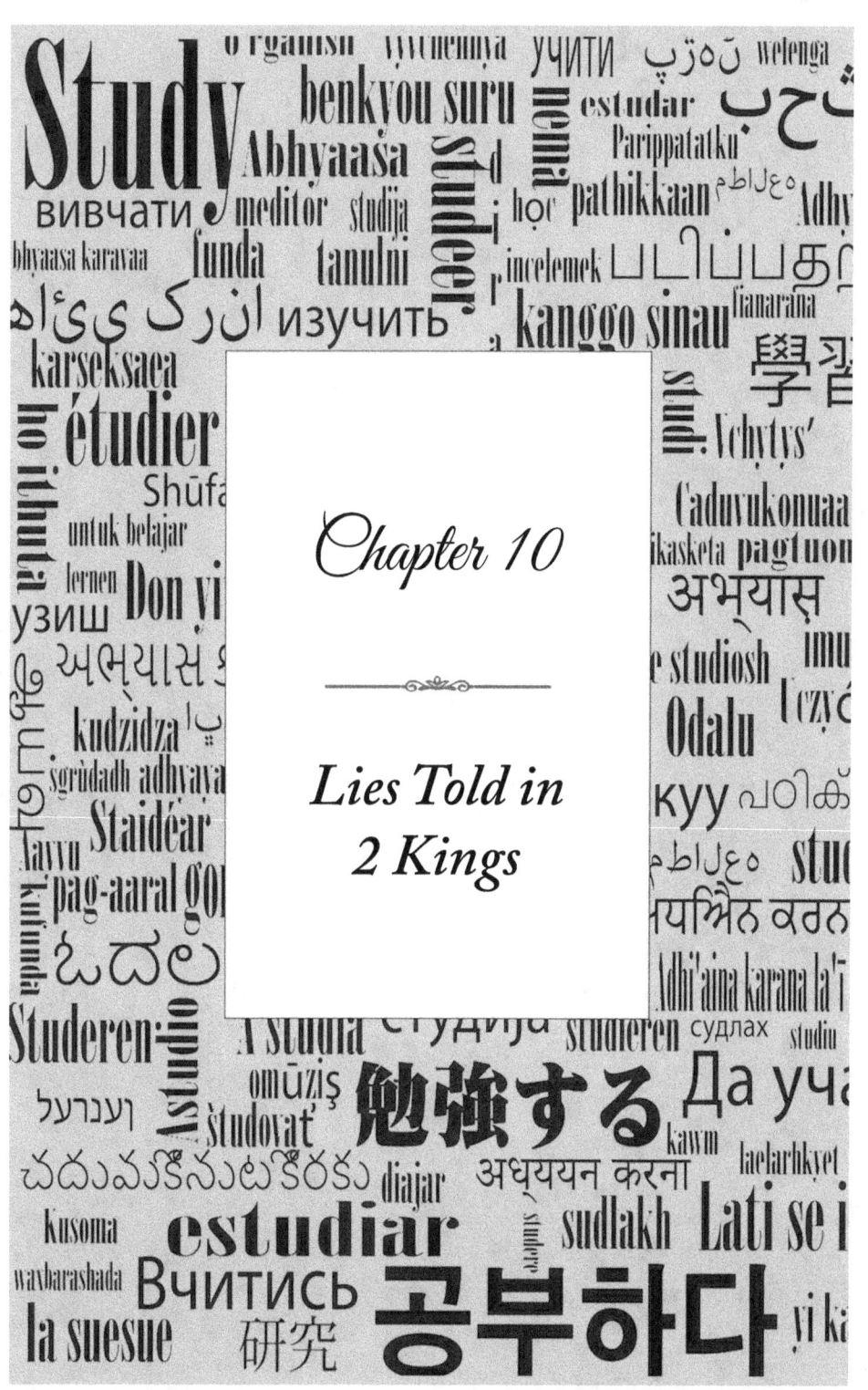

# Chapter 10

## Lies Told in 2 Kings

Gehazi's Lie: Through God's instructions to Elisha, Naaman, a Syrian, was healed of leprosy. Out of a new belief and reverence for the God of Israel, Naaman vowed to no longer sacrifice to other gods. He offered to give gifts to Elisha out of gratitude for his healing. Elisha flatly refused, saying as long as God lives, he would not take a gift. Naaman's new change of heart increased as he had experienced the integrity of a true servant of God.

Yet, Elisha's servant Gehazi lied to Naaman in an act of materialistic greed. Gehazi followed Naaman as he left, and devised a plot to gain what Elisha had turned down. When Gehazi stopped Naaman, he asked Gehazi if all was well. **2 Kings 5:22:** *"'Everything is all right,' Gehazi answered. 'My master sent me to say, "Two young men from the company of the prophets have just come to me from the hill country of Ephraim. Please give them a talent of silver and two sets of clothing."'"* Naaman gave Gehazi what he asked for, and Gehazi took the items for himself. When Gehazi returned, Elisha asked him if this was a time to receive money or material gain. Then Gehazi was cursed with the same leprosy from which Naaman was healed.

---

King Jehu's Lie: Jehu was divinely appointed king by God. King Jehu in his fervor for the Lord gathered all the people together and lied to them in order to identify all the worshipers of Baal, a false god. He pretended to be a Baal worshiper himself. **2 Kings 10:19:** *"Now summon all the prophets of Baal, all his servants and all his priests. See that no one is missing, because I am going to hold a great sacrifice for Baal. Anyone who fails to come will no longer live.' But Jehu was acting deceptively in order to destroy the servants of Baal."* King Jehu had the Baal worshipers killed and ridded Baal itself from Israel.

---

The King's Official's Lie: The king of Assyria had his officials lie to the people in an attempt to turn them against King Hezekiah. They made grand offers of gifts to all. **2 Kings 18:31-32:** *"Do not listen to Hezekiah. This is what the king of Assyria says: Make peace with me and come out to me. Then each of you will eat fruit from your own vine and fig tree and drink water from your own cistern, until I come and take you to a land like your own—a land of grain and new wine, a land of bread and vineyards, a land of olive trees and honey. Choose life and not death! Do not listen to Hezekiah, for he is misleading you when he says, 'The Lord will deliver us.'"* It is true that the king of Assyria had triumphed in the past, but he now boasted of beating the nation that trusted in God. The king of Assyria lost that battle. An angel of the Lord left that king's army all dead corpses. While the king was worshiping in the house of his god Nisrok, his two sons stabbed him with a sword and escaped to Armenia. Another son took his place and reigned as king.

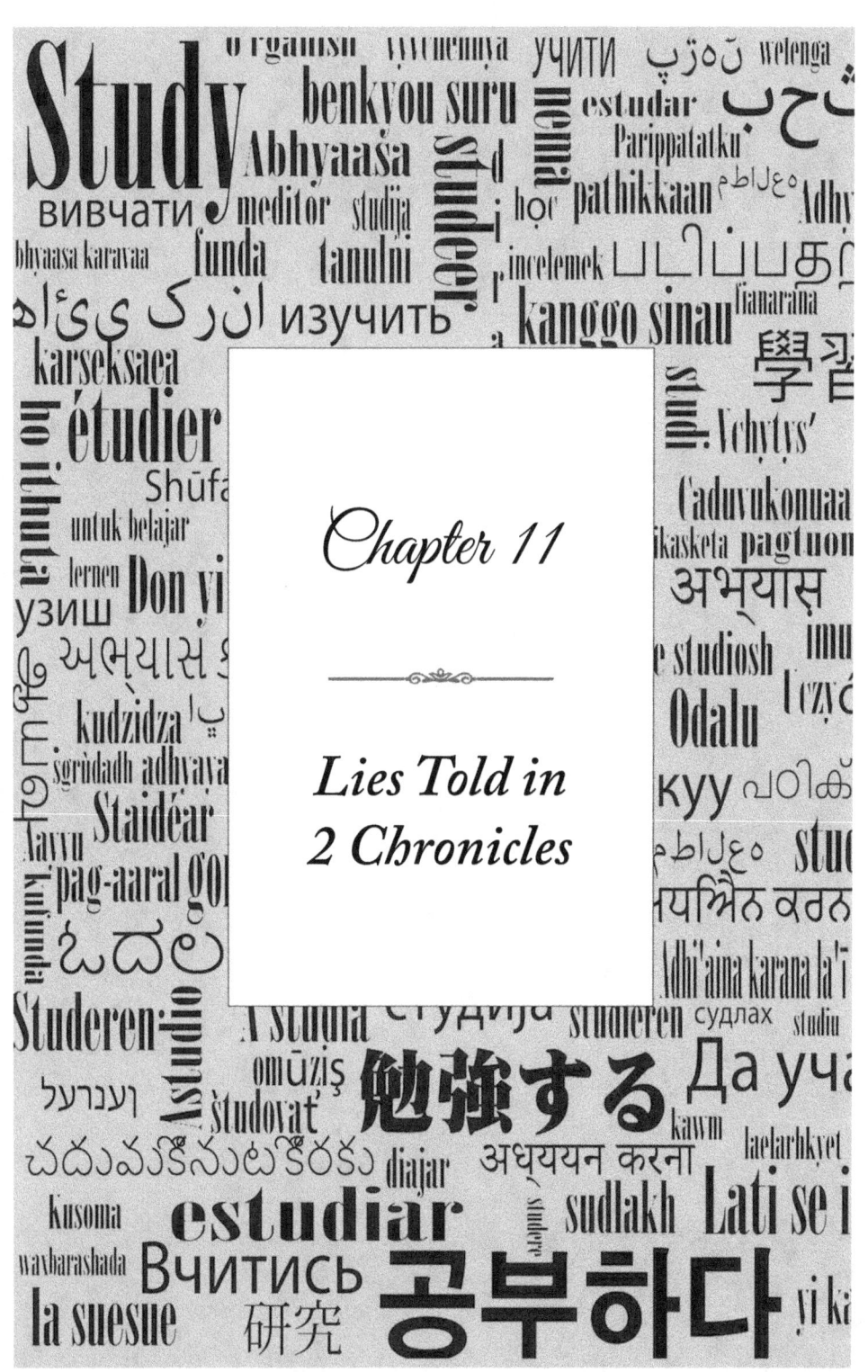

Chapter 11

Lies Told in
2 Chronicles

Prophets' Lies: The two Books of Chronicles record the genealogy and past events that occurred thus far in the history of Israel. It includes a narrative of events from the first chapter of 1 Kings. It tells of the lies the prophets told King Ahab and what occurred as a result. **2 Chronicles 18:5:** *"So the king of Israel brought together the prophets—four hundred men—and asked them, 'Shall we go to war against Ramoth Gilead, or shall I not?' 'Go,' they answered, 'for God will give it into the king's hand.'"* **2 Chronicles 18:11:** *"All the other prophets were prophesying the same thing. 'Attack Ramoth Gilead and be victorious,' they said, 'for the Lord will give it into the king's hand.'"* **2 Chronicles 18:14:** *"When he arrived, the king asked him, 'Micaiah, shall we go to war against Ramoth Gilead, or shall I not?' 'Attack and be victorious,' he answered, 'for they will be given into your hand.'"* Also chronicled is the statement that the Lord had put a lying spirit in the mouths of the king's prophets.

---

Sennacherib's Lie: **2 Chronicles 32:15:** *"Now do not let Hezekiah deceive you and mislead you like this. Do not believe him, for no god of any nation or kingdom has been able to deliver his people from my hand or the hand of my predecessors. How much less will your god deliver you from my hand!"* Sennacherib, king of Assyria, is calling Hezekiah a deceiver and a liar when in fact he, Sennacherib, is the lying deceiver.

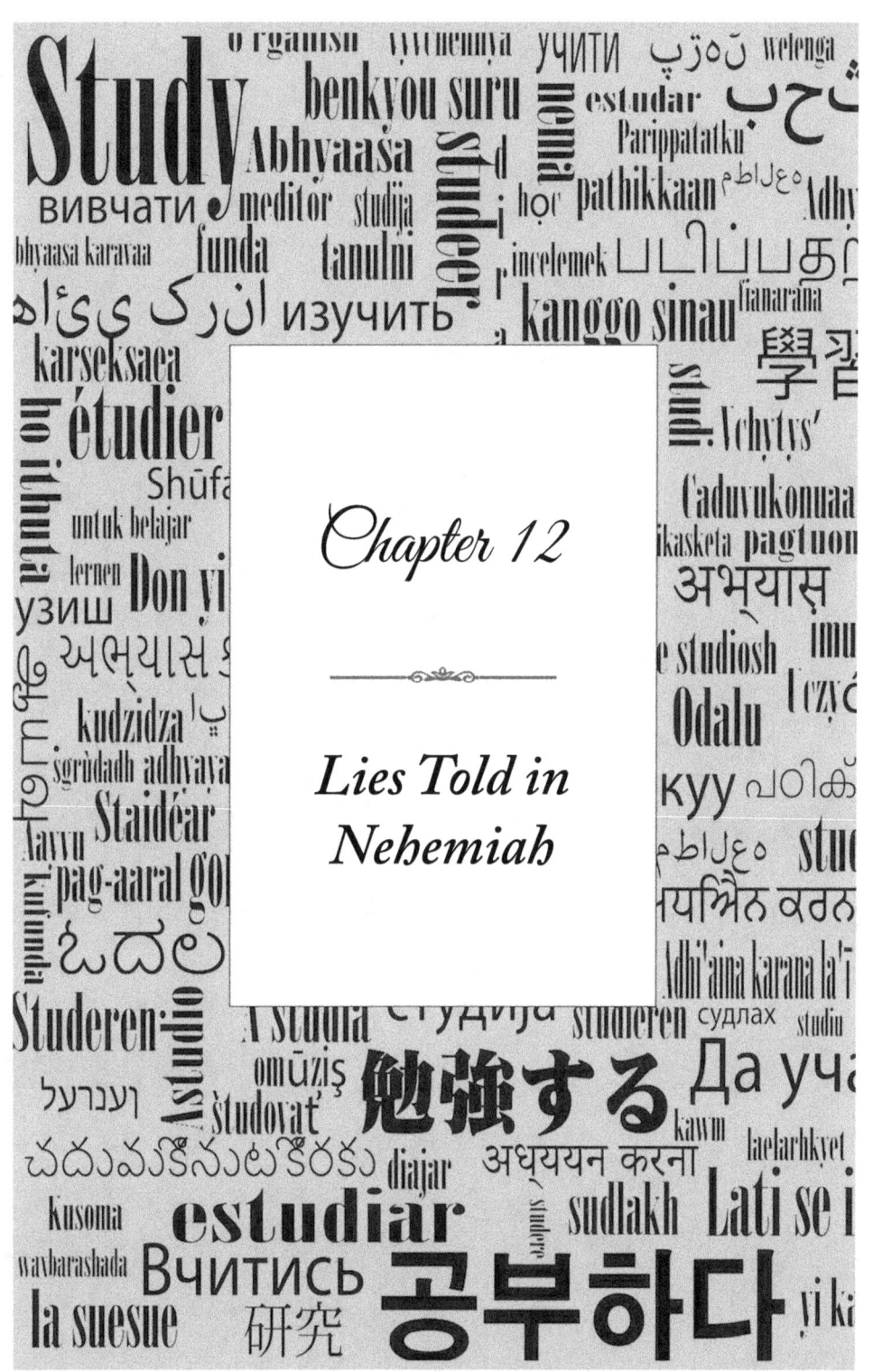

Chapter 12

Lies Told in Nehemiah

Hired Prophets' Lies: **Nehemiah 6:6-7:** *"in which was written: 'It is reported among the nations—and Geshem says it is true—that you and the Jews are plotting to revolt, and therefore you are building the wall. Moreover, according to these reports you are about to become their king and have even appointed prophets to make this proclamation about you in Jerusalem: "There is a king in Judah!" Now this report will get back to the king; so come, let us meet together.'"*

*Is it better to trust a respected friend or a hired consultant?*

**Nehemiah 6:10:** *"One day I went to the house of Shemaiah son of Delaiah, the son of Mehetabel, who was shut in at his home. He said, 'Let us meet in the house of God, inside the temple, and let us close the temple doors, because men are coming to kill you—by night they are coming to kill you.'"*

These three verses of Scripture encompass several lies told by hired prophets.

# Chapter 13

*Liars in Job*

Although Job disagreed with the erroneous, judgmental opinions of his friends and called them *"forgers of lies"* (Job 13:4)—like those who "hammer" at their opinions and pounds them into you as truth—in the end, God also disagreed with Job's friends.

Chapter 14

Mentions in Psalms

Although there are no direct lies in the Book of Psalms, there are mentions in several verses about the consequences of lying and what God thinks of liars. Specific chapter and verses are cited in the Appendix.

# Chapter 15

## Mentions in Proverbs

As with Psalms, there are no direct lies in the Book of Proverbs, but there are numerous mentions regarding why lying is wrong and why we all are admonished not to lie. See specific chapter and verses in the Appendix.

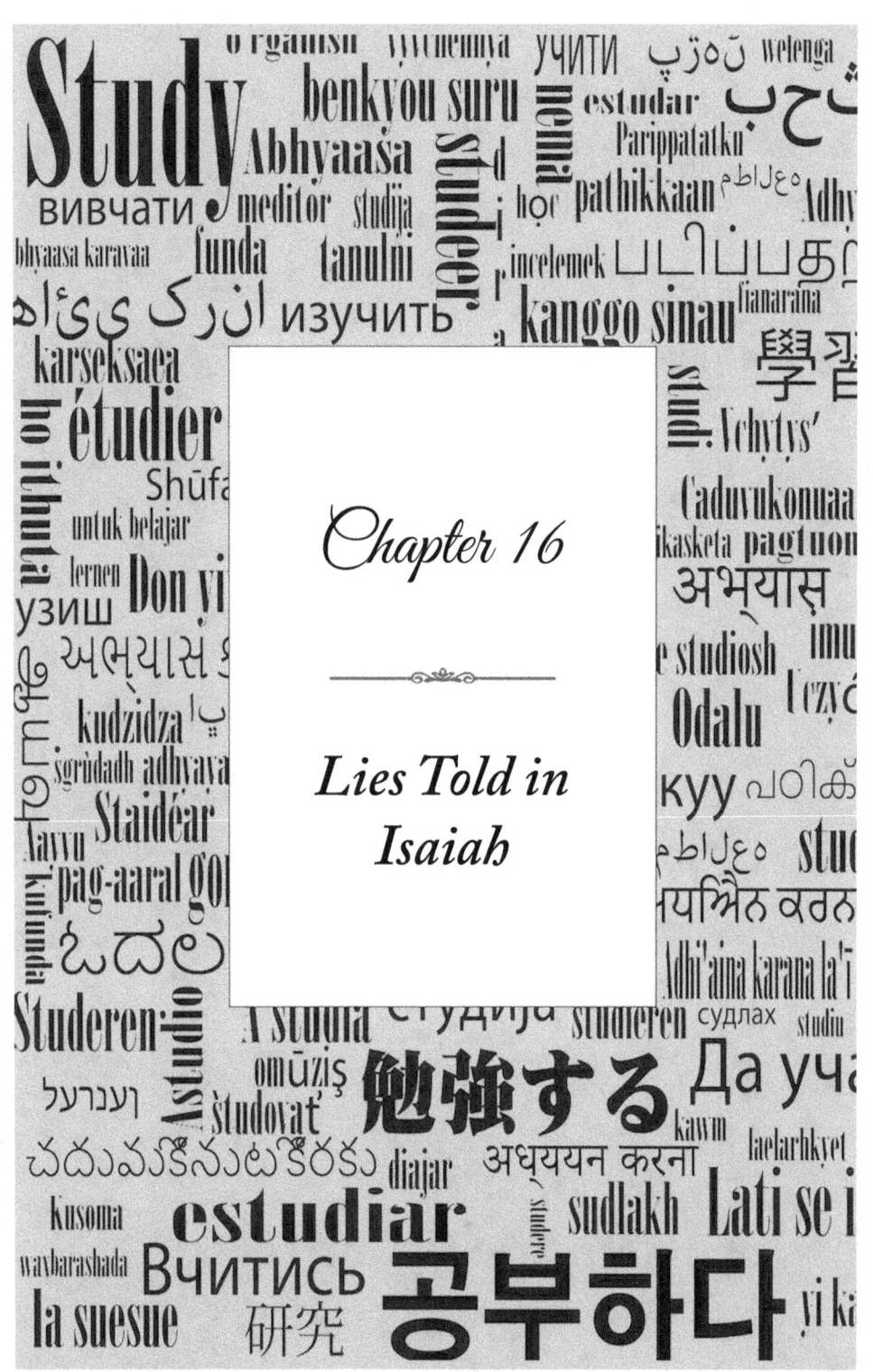

*Chapter 16*

*Lies Told in Isaiah*

Army Commander's Lie: We learned of this next story in Chapter 10, Lies in 2 Kings. The king of Assyria sent the commander of his humongous army to speak to the people of Israel with threats, manipulative boasting, and lying. **Isaiah 36:6-8:** *"Look, I know you are depending on Egypt, that splintered reed of a staff, which pierces the hand of anyone who leans on it! Such is Pharaoh king of Egypt to all who depend on him. But if you say to me, 'We are depending on the Lord our God'—isn't he the one whose high places and altars Hezekiah removed, saying to Judah and Jerusalem, 'You must worship before this altar'? Come now, make a bargain with my master, the king of Assyria: I will give you two thousand horses—if you can put riders on them!'"* **Isaiah 36:10:** *"Furthermore, have I come to attack and destroy this land without the Lord? The Lord himself told me to march against this country and destroy it."*

Rabshakeh's Lie: Then Rabshakeh stood up and spoke in a loud voice to all the Jews in their own language. **Isaiah 36:14-18:** *"This is what the king says: Do not let Hezekiah deceive you. He cannot deliver you! Do not let Hezekiah persuade you to trust in the Lord when he says, 'The Lord will surely deliver us; this city will not be given into the hand of the king of Assyria.' Do not listen to Hezekiah. This is what the king of Assyria says: Make peace with me and come out to me. Then each of you will eat fruit from your own vine and fig tree and drink water from your own cistern, until I come and take you to a land like your own—a land of grain and new wine, a land of bread and vineyards. Do not let Hezekiah mislead you when he says, 'The Lord will deliver us.' Have the gods of any nations ever delivered their lands from the hand of the king of Assyria?"*

**Isaiah 36:20:** *"Who of all the gods of these countries have been able to save their lands from me? How then can the Lord deliver Jerusalem from my hand?"* The people did not answer a single word. A messenger was later sent to Hezekiah with more lies.

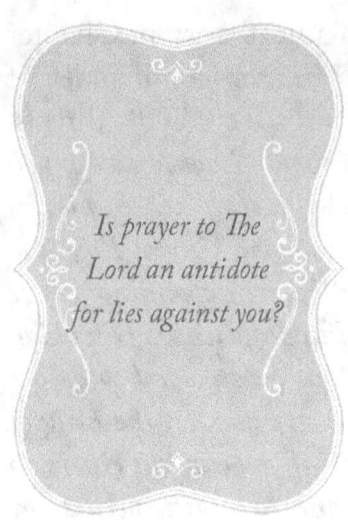

*Is prayer to The Lord an antidote for lies against you?*

**Isaiah 37:10:** *"Say to Hezekiah king of Judah: Do not let the god you depend on deceive you when he says, 'Jerusalem will not be given into the hands of the king of Assyria.'"* Hezekiah's response was simply to pray to the Lord. The end result was the king of Assyria and his army were dead.

---

Lies by Misleading Leaders: **Isaiah 56:12:** *"'Come,' each one cries, 'let me get wine! Let us drink our fill of beer! And tomorrow will be like today, or even far better.'"* This is the lie told of lazy yet greedy, wicked, and ignorant leaders who are misleading others. God responds that this is not so, lies will always come to an end.

---

Included in the Appendix are instances when lying, liars, and lies are mentioned and the impact they have on people targeted with lies as well as the people who lie.

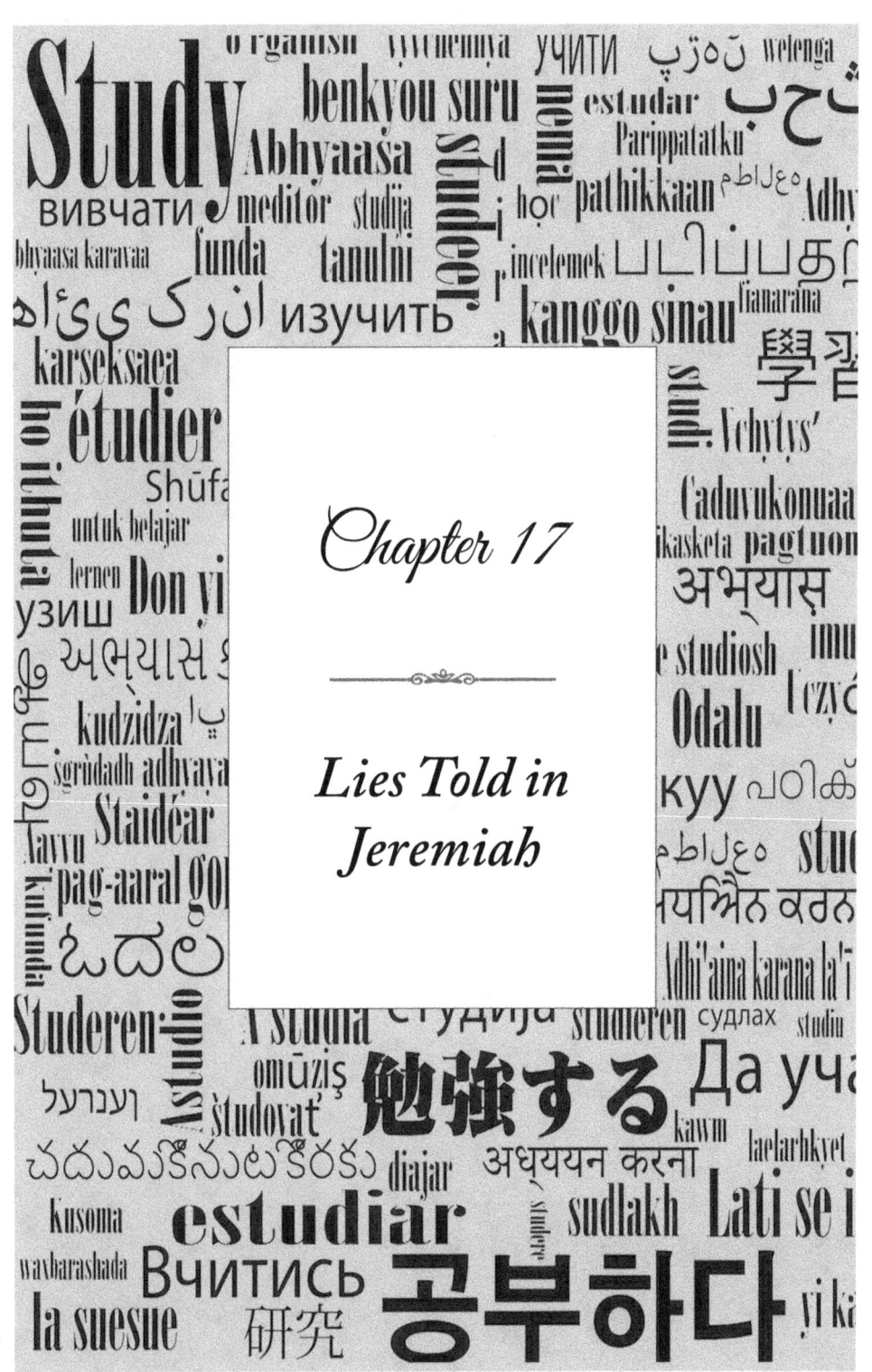

*Chapter 17*

*Lies Told in Jeremiah*

**Hananiah's Lies:** The prophet Jeremiah had prophesied a harsh truth that all the nations were to be yoked to serve Nebuchadnezzar, the king of Babylon. Jeremiah also prophesied that the Lord said anyone who says otherwise would be prophesying lies. Later on in that same year, another prophet named Hananiah spoke to Jeremiah in the house of the Lord, in the presence of the priest and the people. He prophesied saying He would break the yoke of Babylon from the people. **Jeremiah 28:2-4:** *"This is what the Lord Almighty, the God of Israel, says: 'I will break the yoke of the king of Babylon. Within two years I will bring back to this place all the articles of the Lord's house that Nebuchadnezzar king of Babylon removed from here and took to Babylon. I will also bring back to this place Jehoiachin son of Jehoiakim king of Judah and all the other exiles from Judah who went to Babylon,' declares the Lord, 'for I will break the yoke of the king of Babylon.'"*

Even Jeremiah had hoped it was true, but it wasn't. Jeremiah spoke to all saying a prophet prophesying peace will only be considered a word from God when it comes to pass. But Hananiah continued to speak. **Jeremiah 28:11:** *"and he [Hananiah] said before all the people, 'This is what the Lord says: "In the same way I will break the yoke of Nebuchadnezzar king of Babylon off the neck of all the nations within two years." At this, the prophet Jeremiah went on his way."* Jeremiah left. God sent Jeremiah back to Hananiah and said to tell him what thus said the Lord of hosts, the God of Israel. Jeremiah told Hananiah that God had not sent him; therefore, he made the people trust in a lie. Through Jeremiah, the Lord also said that Hananiah would die that year because he taught rebellion against the Lord. Hananiah died that same year in the seventh month.

---

**Captain of the Guard's Lie:** The captain of the guard in the territory of Benjamin falsely accused Jeremiah of joining the Babylonians because of his prophecies. **Jeremiah 37:13:** *"But when he reached the Benjamin Gate, the captain of the guard, whose name was Irijah* *son of Shelemiah, the son of Hananiah; arrested him and said, 'You are deserting to the Babylonians!'"* Jeremiah then said it was not true, denying the false accusation. Irijah did not believe Jeremiah and took him to the princes. In their anger toward Jeremiah, they beat him and put him in prison. The king himself, Zedekiah, took Jeremiah from the prison and secretly invited him to his house. The king asked Jeremiah if there was a word from the Lord. Jeremiah did not change his previous prophecy to suit the king. Nor did he change it to get out of his imprisonment. Wherefore, Jeremiah remained in prison.

---

Officials' Lies: Later on as the officials recapped the prophesying of Jeremiah, soon came more false accusations against him. **Jeremiah 38:4:** *"Then the officials said to the king, 'This man should be put to death. He is discouraging the soldiers who are left in this city, as well as all the people, by the things he is saying to them. This man is not seeking the good of these people but their ruin.'"* They took Jeremiah and placed him in a muddy dungeon where he was to starve to death. Once the king was made aware, he had Jeremiah secretly moved from the dungeon. In time, Jeremiah was set free by the prison guard's captain.

---

Gedaliah's Lie: An army captain named Johanan warned Gedaliah, the governor, that the king of the Ammonites had sent Ishmael to kill him. Johanan spoke to Gedaliah secretly, offering to instead kill Ishmael. **Jeremiah 40:16:** *"But Gedaliah son of Ahikam said to Johanan son of Kareah, 'Don't do such a thing! What you are saying* *about Ishmael is not true.'"* Unfortunately, Gedaliah spoke falsely as he accused Johanan of speaking falsely. It cost him his life, because truthfully Ishmael was sent to kill him, and he did. Ishmael killed Gedaliah while they were sitting down eating together. Ishmael and the men with him unsuspectingly killed all the men who were with Gedaliah.

Ishmael's Lie: Numerous men came to the house of the Lord mourning in worship. Ishmael pretended to be crying in worship with the others. **Jeremiah 41:6:** *"Ishmael son of Nethaniah went out from Mizpah to meet them, weeping as he went. When he met them, he said, 'Come to Gedaliah son of Ahikam.'"* Ishmael had already killed Gedaliah. He told the tricky lie to mislead them to their death.

---

The People's Lies: The people asked Jeremiah to pray to God for the direction they should go. **Jeremiah 42:5-6:** *"Then they said to Jeremiah, 'May the Lord be a true and faithful witness against us if we do not act in accordance with everything the Lord your God sends you to tell us. Whether it is favorable or unfavorable, we will obey the Lord our God, to whom we are sending you, so that it will go well with us, for we will obey the Lord our God.'"* After Jeremiah declared what God said to do, the people instead disobeyed. In disobedience, they were now certain to die in the place they desired to go.

Once again Jeremiah is falsely accused of prophesying lies. **Jeremiah 43:2-3:** *"Azariah son of Hoshaiah and Johanan son of Kareah and all the arrogant men said to Jeremiah, 'You are lying! The Lord our God has not sent you to say, "You must not go to Egypt to settle there." But Baruch son of Neriah is inciting you against us to hand us over to the Babylonians, so they may kill us or carry us into exile to Babylon.'"* So the people disobeyed the voice of the Lord, resulting in grave consequences.

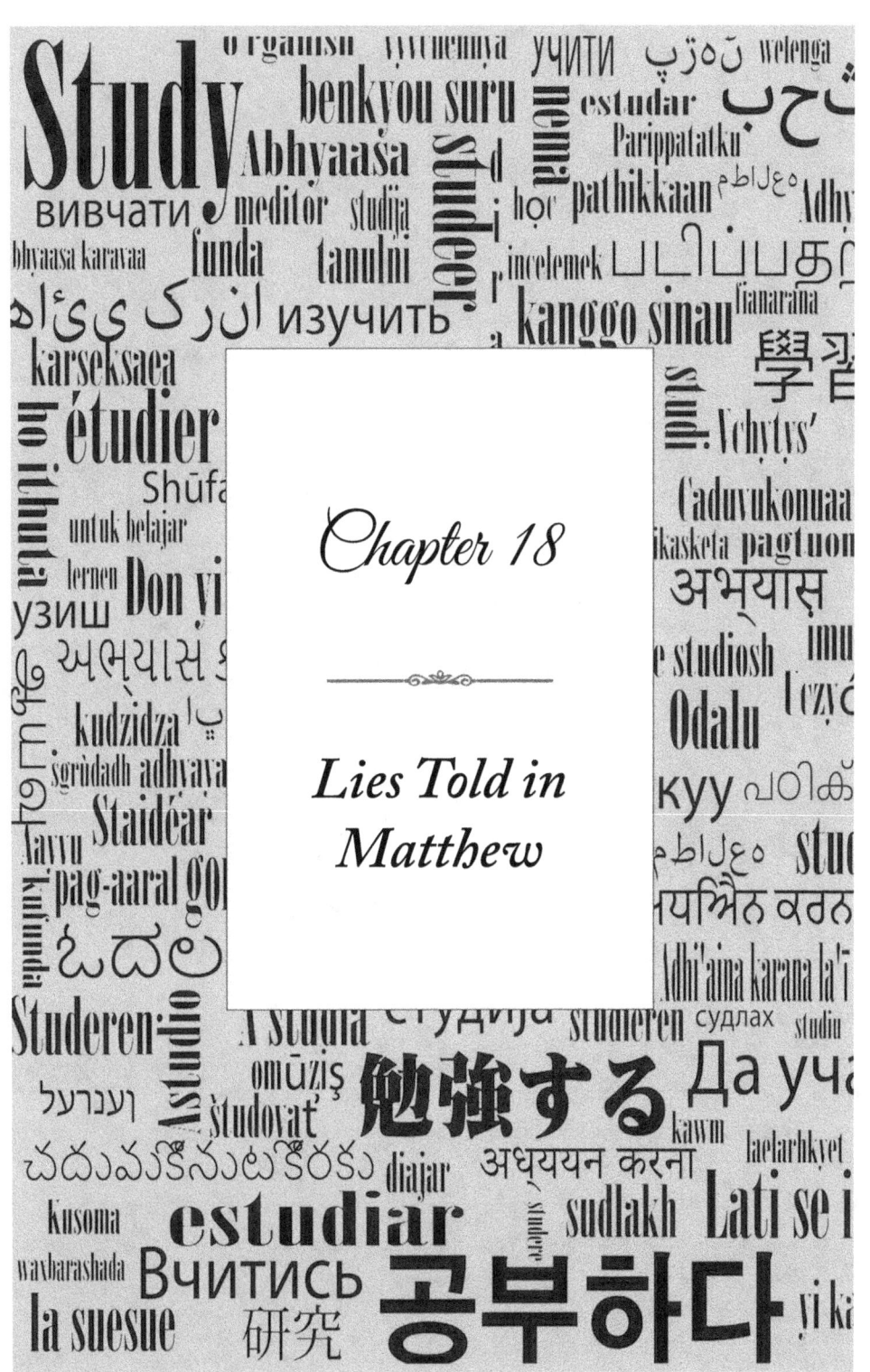

*Chapter 18*

*Lies Told in Matthew*

Herod's Lie: Jesus Christ was born in Bethlehem. When Herod, the Roman king, heard of Jesus' birth and His purpose, he ordered a search to find Jesus. **Matthew 2:8: *"He sent them to Bethlehem and said, 'Go and search carefully for the child. As soon as you find him, report to me, so that I too may go and worship him.'"*** Herod had lied and had no intentions of worshiping Jesus. Herod made this request to wise men who were following a bright star—a cosmic phenomenon actually historically noted.

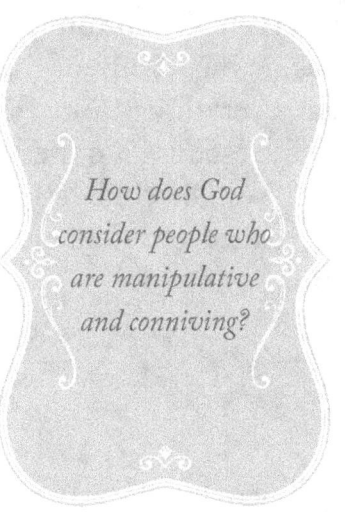

*How does God consider people who are manipulative and conniving?*

That star led them to find the house where the Child was with His earthly parents, Mary and Joseph. The men were warned by God in a dream not to return to Herod. They instead returned to their own home destinations. Afterward, an angel appeared to Joseph in a dream and instructed him to flee to Egypt with the young Child and His mother, because Herod sought to kill the Child, Jesus. They stayed in Egypt until that particular Herod died.

---

Satan's Lie: When Jesus was about 30 years of age and at the beginning of His earthly ministry, God led Jesus by the Spirit into the wilderness to be tempted by the devil. Jesus had fasted forty days and forty nights and was hungry. He encountered a first, second, then third temptation. On the third temptation, the devil took Jesus up onto a high mountain and showed Him all the kingdoms of the world and the splendor of them. **Matthew 4:9: *"All this I will give you,' he said, 'if you will bow down and worship me.'"*** The father of lies tempts Jesus with the same lie that has deceived many, causing a perpetually bottomless greed that will never be fulfilled. The devil has no ownership of the earth to give it. The earth belongs to God and everything in it. The devil offers a worldly system that entices. Jesus' response is our example to any temptations from the enemy—the Word of God. Jesus told the devil, *"It is written"* to worship and serve the Lord God only (see Matthew 4:4,7,10). Then the devil left him.

Pharisees' Lies: Jesus traveled around healing people of every disease and every sickness. Jesus cast out demons and worked miracles such as had never been seen before in Israel. **Matthew 9:34: *"But the Pharisees said, 'It is by the prince of demons that he drives out demons.'"*** The Pharisees' oxymoronic lie was basically that Jesus cast out devils with the help of the chief devil. Jesus did not respond to this lie; He continued preaching and healing. Yet, Jesus did not forget. Later, the lie was repeated by the local religious leaders because the people were amazed at Jesus. **Matthew 12:24: *"But when the Pharisees heard this, they said, 'It is only by Beelzebul, the prince of demons, that this fellow drives out demons.'"*** At this time, Jesus responds with a question. He says to them that if Satan casts out Satan, he is divided against himself and his kingdom will not stand (see Matthew 12:26). Additionally, Jesus told the Pharisees that He casts out devils by the Spirit of God.

Peter's Lies: After Jesus was betrayed, He was taken to the high priest, Caiaphas, and arrested. Peter followed Him to learn what would happen to Jesus. Later in the courtyard of the palace, a young girl came to Peter and said he was one of the ones who followed Jesus. His response to her was to lie in denial. **Matthew 26:70:** *"But he denied it before them all. 'I don't know what you're talking about,' he said."* As Peter walked farther, another young woman saw him and also said that Peter was with Jesus. Peter lied again. **Matthew 26:72:** *"He denied it again, with an oath, 'I don't know the man!'"* A little while afterward, others came to Peter saying surely he was one of the ones with Jesus, and his accent proves it. Peter then lied a third time. **Matthew 26:74:** *"Then he began to call down curses, and he swore to them, 'I don't know the man!' Immediately a rooster crowed."* Peter then remembered what Jesus had said to him earlier—that Peter would deny Him three times before the cock crowed. Peter left, crying bitterly.

---

Soldiers' Lie: Jesus the Christ was crucified and died. At the beginning of dawn three days later, Jesus had risen from the dead—He was no longer in the tomb where He was laid. When His absence was evident, the chief priests and elders paid a large amount of money to the soldiers who kept guard of Jesus' sepulcher. **Matthew 28:13:** *"telling them, 'You are to say, "His disciples came during the night and stole him away while we were asleep."'"* The soldiers took the money and lied as instructed.

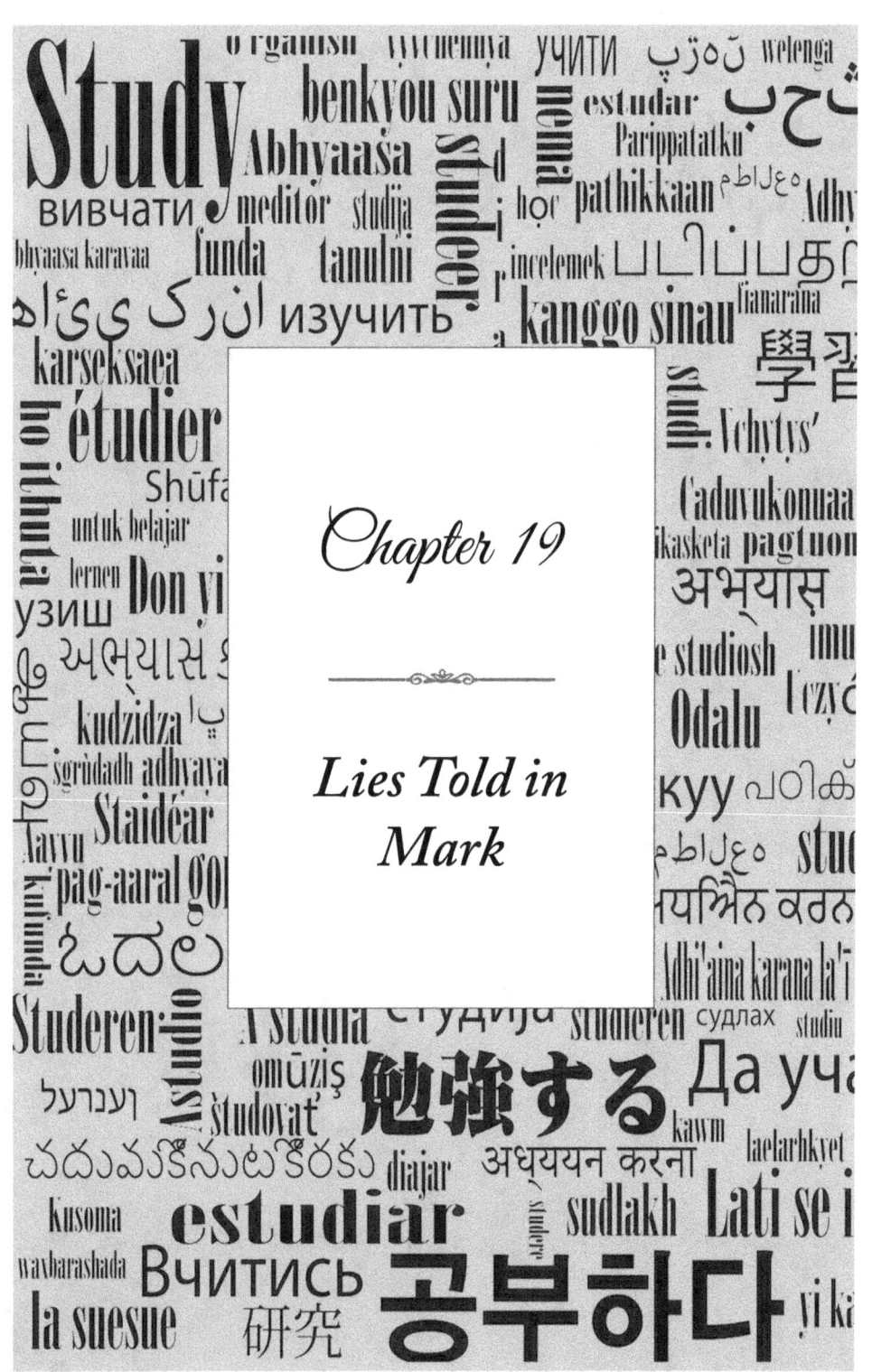

# Chapter 19

## Lies Told in Mark

Family and Friends' Lie: Sometimes family and friends fail to understand our plans or purpose in life; many times they are well meaning, but wrong. This occurs especially when our plans are out of the norm. Some family and friends' erroneous valuation of Jesus' ministry caused them to lie about His actions. Jesus experienced this when His family and friends came to town seeking to contain His efforts. **Mark 3:21:** *"When his family heard about this, they went to take charge of him, for they said, 'He is out of his mind.'"*

---

Pharisees' Lies: The New Testament Gospels share some of the same stories or occurrences; though written differently as any version of a story would be when told by different people. After all is said, though, the facts remain. Just as recorded in the Book of Matthew, Mark shares the same occurrence: **Mark 3:22:** *"And the teachers of the law who came down from Jerusalem said, 'He is possessed by Beelzebul! By the prince of demons he is driving out demons.'"* They continued to lie about Jesus. **Mark 3:30:** *"He said this because they were saying, 'He has an impure spirit.'"*

---

Peter's Lies: Mark also tells his version of Peter disowning Jesus. **Mark 14:29:** *"Peter declared, 'Even if all fall away, I will not.'"* Jesus again assured Peter that truthfully he would disown Him not once, but three times. Then Peter spoke the lie vehemently, believing his own words to be positively true, in spite of what Jesus said. **Mark 14:31:** *"But Peter insisted emphatically, 'Even if I have to die with you, I will never disown you.' And all the others said the same."*

Just as told in the Book of Matthew, Mark also tells of the young girl who told others that Peter was with Jesus. **Mark 14:68:** ***"But he denied it. 'I don't know or understand what you're talking about,' he said, and went out into the entryway."*** A servant girl also said Peter was one of them with Jesus. **Mark 14:70-71:** ***"Again he denied it. After a little while, those standing near said to Peter, 'Surely you are one of them, for you are a Galilean.' He began to call down curses, and he swore to them, 'I don't know this man you're talking about.'"*** Just as Jesus said would happen, happened. When Peter thought about how he lied, disowned, and abandoned Jesus, he cried.

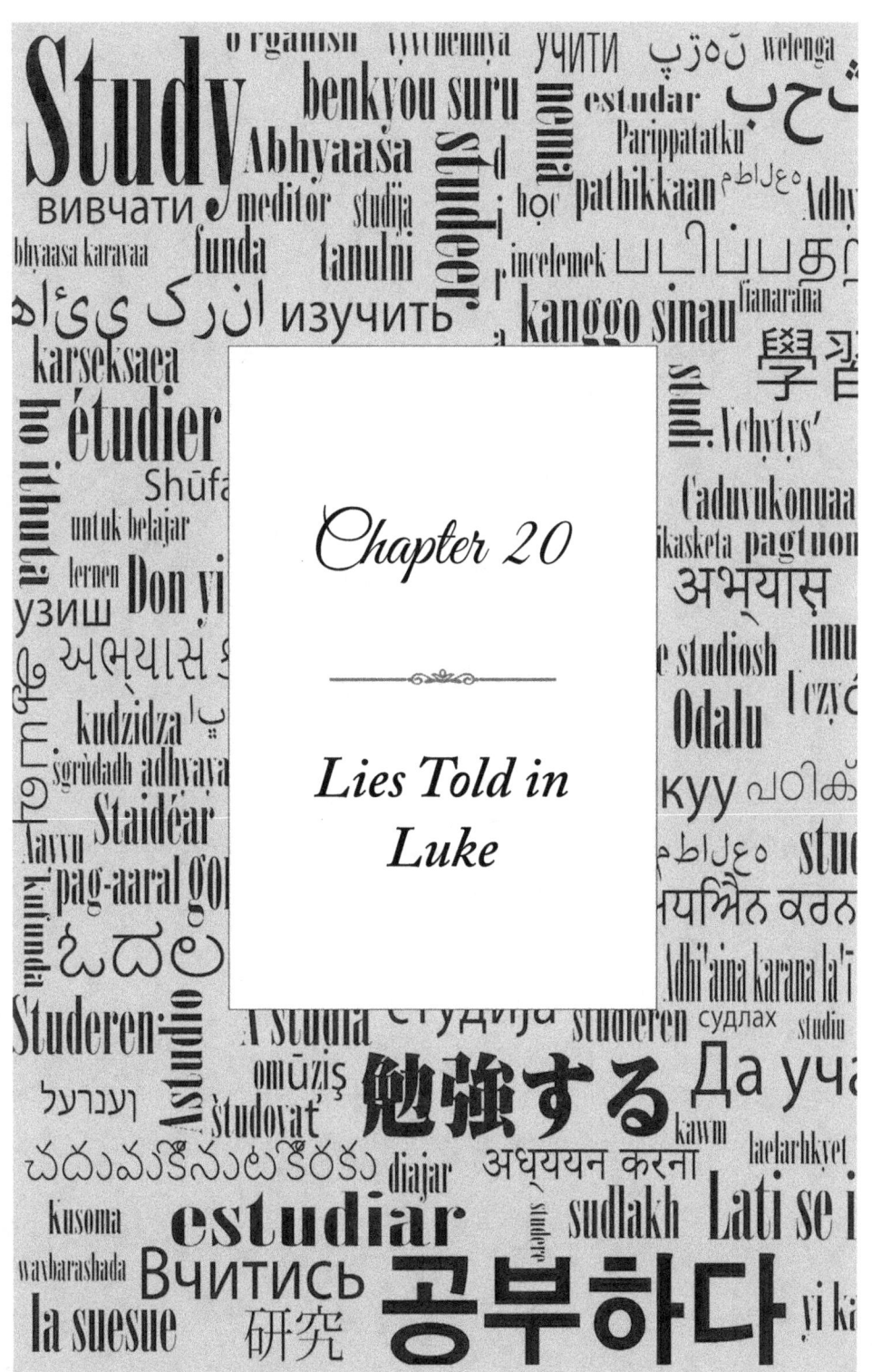

*Chapter 20*

*Lies Told in Luke*

**The Devil's Lie:** The Book of Luke was written by Luke, a physician of detail; it also tells of Jesus being tempted by the devil. **Luke 4:6-7:** *"And he* **[the devil]** *said to him, 'I will give you all their authority and splendor; it has been given to me, and I can give it to anyone I want to. If you worship me, it will all be yours.'"* The devil is lying about his power and authority to give. He is not all-powerful and deceives many into believing he has the power and authority of God. Again, Jesus' response is our example to any temptations from the enemy—the Word of God. Jesus told the devil, *"It is written"* to worship and serve the Lord God only. After several attempts to tempt Jesus, the devil left, only for a while.

---

**The People's Lie:** Luke also tells of some others who said Jesus casts out devils, by the devil. The people were amazed and had never seen those who couldn't speak, suddenly start speaking. The tendency is to be frightened instead of excited when out of the norm happens. **Luke 11:15:** *"But some of them said, 'By Beelzebul, the prince of demons, he is driving out demons.'"* Jesus responded powerfully against the lie (see Luke 11:17-23).

---

**Peter's Lies:** Just as told in the other three Gospels (Matthew, Mark and John), Peter disowned Jesus on three different occasions just as Jesus said he would. **Luke 22:57-58:** *"But he denied it. 'Woman, I don't know him,' he said. And a little later someone else saw him and said, 'You also are one of them.' 'Man, I am not!' Peter replied."* **Luke 22:60:** *"Peter replied, 'Man, I don't know what you're talking about!' Just as*

***he was speaking, the rooster crowed.****"* After saying he would even go to prison or die for Jesus, Peter lied three times denying he even knew Him.

---

The Multitude's Lie: They took Jesus to Pilate. **Luke 23:2: *"And they began to accuse him, saying, 'We have found this man subverting our nation. He opposes payment of taxes to Caesar, and claims to be Messiah, a king.'"*** There were several lying accusations against Jesus, including the lie that He did not pay His taxes.

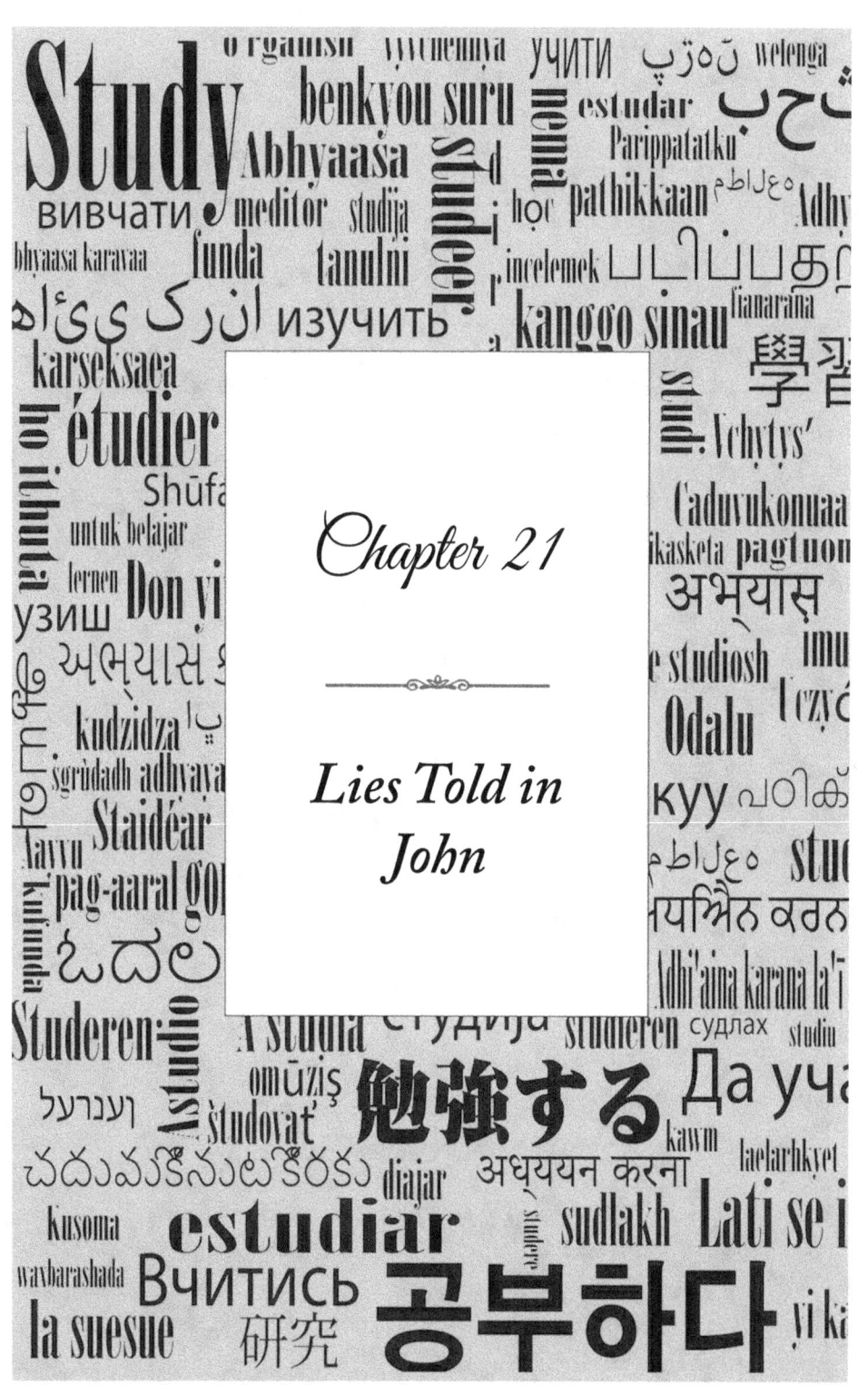

# Chapter 21

## Lies Told in John

Nonbelievers' Lie: During the Feast of Tabernacles, the Jews wondered where Jesus was. **John 7:12: *"Among the crowds there was widespread whispering about him. Some said, 'He is a good man.' Others replied, 'No, he deceives the people.'"*** Those who did not believe Jesus lied about Him continuously. They believed the words Jesus spoke were false and deceptive. What do you believe?

---

The People's Lie: Jesus went into the temple and taught. The Jews were amazed at His doctrine and knowledge, although He had no formal education. As part of Jesus' response, He asked why none of them kept the law of the Letters they learned, given by Moses. He asked them why they tried to kill Him. **John 7:20: *"'You are demon-possessed,' the crowd answered. 'Who is trying to kill you?'"*** They lied to Jesus because He angered them with the truth. Also, they did seek to kill Jesus, but they could not yet do so. When the time would come for His death, He would allow it.

The Pharisees' Lie: The Pharisees spoke falsely of Jesus again. **John 8:13: *"The Pharisees challenged him, 'Here you are, appearing as your own witness; your testimony is not valid.'"***

The Jews' Lies: The Pharisees were calling Jesus a liar as He spoke of who He is. And again the Jews made false accusations against Jesus. **John 8:48: *"The Jews answered him, 'Aren't we right in saying that you are a Samaritan and demon-possessed?'"*** Of course Jesus answers truthfully that He does not have a devil. Calling Jesus a Samaritan was akin to name-calling—to reduce His character—and was not worth His response. They knew He was not a Samaritan. Jesus says whoever obeys His words will never see death. **John 8:52: *"At this they exclaimed, 'Now we know that you are demon-possessed! Abraham died and so did the prophets, yet you say that whoever obeys*** *your word will never taste death.'"* The Jews failed to understand that Jesus was speaking of the spiritual realm. Jesus later answers them that He is not, as they, a liar.

---

Chief Priests' Lies: Jesus miraculously healed a man blind from birth, and gave him his sight. This occurred on the Sabbath. Many witnessed this marvelous miracle and asked Him to tell of it to some Pharisees. The Pharisees showed no regard for the miracle, nor regard for the man healed of blindness. **John 9:16: *"Some of the Pharisees said, 'This man is not from God, for he does not keep the Sabbath.' But others asked, 'How can a sinner perform such signs?' So they were divided."*** They bluntly lied, saying Jesus was not of God simply because He healed someone on the Sabbath. They didn't even believe the man was blind before, until they verified it with his parents. **John 9:24: *"A second time they summoned the man who had been blind. 'Give glory to God by telling the truth,' they said. 'We know this man is a sinner.'"*** The man answered that he doesn't know if Jesus is a sinner or not; but what he does know is that he was blind and now he can see.

---

Jesus said He is the Good Shepherd for all, and He has the power to lay down His life and has the power to take it again; a commandment He received from God, His Father. This truth caused division among the Jews. **John 10:20: *"Many of them said, 'He is demon-possessed and raving mad. Why listen to him?'"*** Others refuted the lies asking if the devil can heal blindness.

Just as recorded in the other Gospels, John tells of Peter lying and denying Jesus. **John 18:17:** *"'You aren't one of this man's disciples too, are you?' she asked Peter. He replied, 'I am not.'"* **John 18:25:** *"Meanwhile, Simon Peter was still standing there warming himself. So they asked him, 'You aren't one of his disciples too, are you?' He denied it, saying, 'I am not.'"* **John 18:27:** *"Again Peter denied it, and at that moment a rooster began to crow."*

*They believed the words Jesus spoke were false and deceptive. What do you believe?*

---

Before Jesus was crucified, there was an exchange of words between Pilate, the Roman governor of the region, and the chief priests, which caused Pilate to have written on the cross of Jesus: "Jesus of Nazareth the King of the Jews." **John 19:21:** *"The chief priests of the Jews protested to Pilate, 'Do not write, "The King of the Jews"; but that this man claimed to be king of the Jews.'"*

Jesus never professed to be King of the Jews, but Pilate's response was that he wrote what he wrote, and it remains.

---

After Jesus was raised from the dead, the third time He revealed Himself to the disciples, they dined with Him. Peter was forgiven for each of the three times he denied Jesus. Now, even after Jesus' resurrection, His sayings were still misconstrued, even among believers. **John 21:23:** *"Because of this, the rumor spread among the believers that this disciple would not die. But Jesus did not say that he would not die; he only said, 'If I want him to remain alive until I return, what is that to you?'"* Then, throughout time, and even today, many have attempted to misconstrue or confuse the true sayings of Jesus. The devil is the source of this confusion. Although countless lies have been told regarding the sayings of Jesus, His sayings—His words—remain truth.

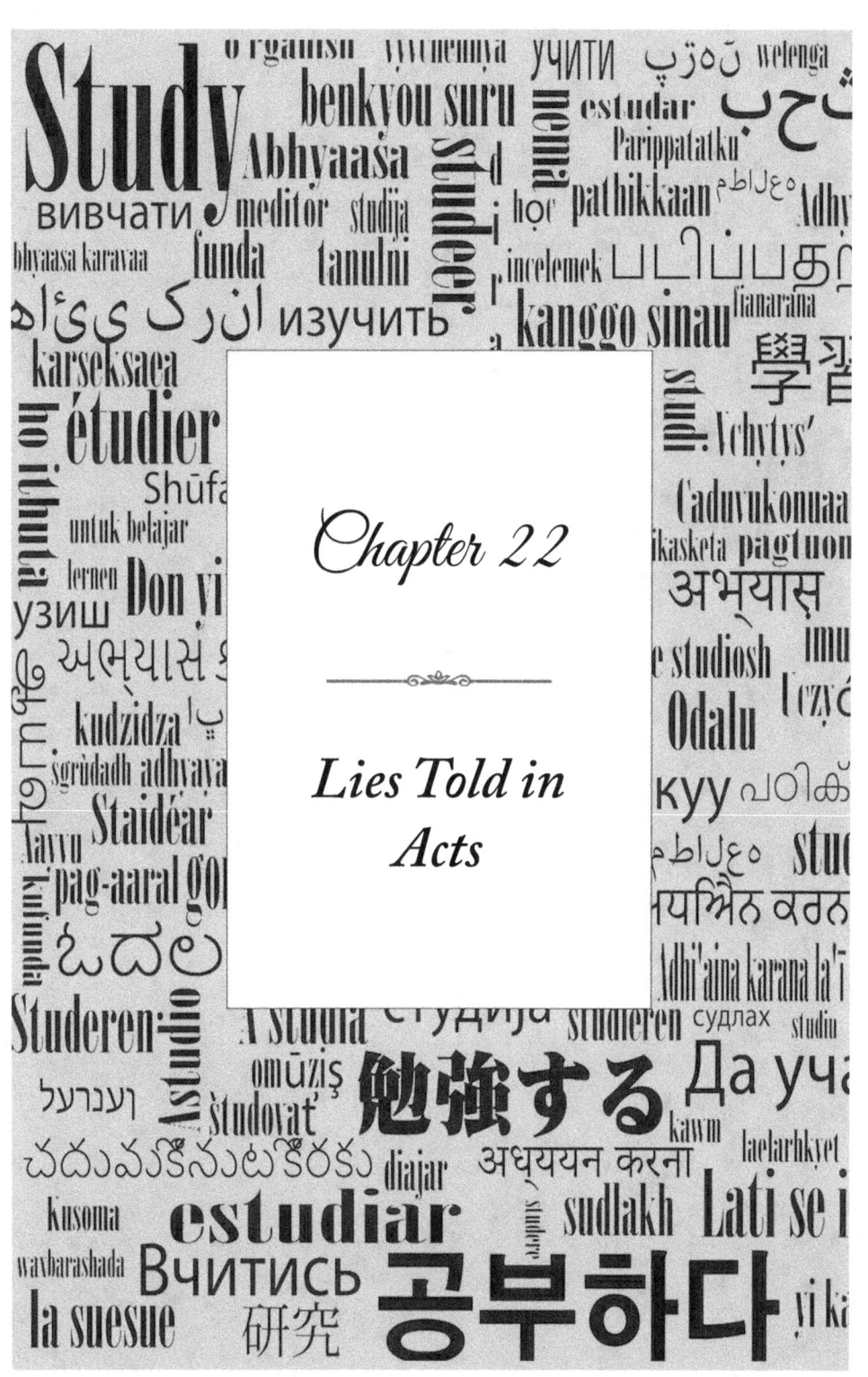

# Chapter 22

## Lies Told in Acts

The People's Lie: On the day of Pentecost, those in one accord were filled with the Holy Spirit and began to speak in other tongues. They were amazingly speaking in languages unknown to them. People from other nations heard them actually speaking in their native languages. They were all amazed and wondered what it all meant. **Acts 2:13:** *"Some, however, made fun of them and said, 'They have had too much wine.'"* Those speaking in other tongues were falsely accused of being drunk.

Ananias and Sapphira's Lie: A multitude of thousands upon thousands believed in Jesus and were of one heart and soul. They came together, even selling possessions to ensure no one lacked or was in need. A man named Ananias and his wife, Sapphira, sold their land, but conspired secretly to keep a portion of the amount for themselves. When Ananias brought the other amount to the apostles, Peter asked him why he had lied to the Holy Spirit, keeping a portion. It was Ananias' money and he had a right to keep it, but he chose to tell a lie. For that lie, Ananias died immediately. Afterward came his wife, Sapphira; unaware of what had occurred, she also lied. **Acts 5:8:** *"Peter asked her, 'Tell me, is this the price you and Ananias got for the land?' 'Yes,' she said, 'that is the price.'"* Peter asked her why they agreed together to test the Spirit of the Lord. Because she lied, she died also and was buried with her husband. A great fear came upon the church as many heard of their deceit. Those who weren't sincere were afraid to join the church.

People in the Synagogue's Lie: The disciples chose seven men who were wise, honest, and filled with the Holy Spirit. They were to take care of the working business of the church. A man full of faith named Stephen was one of those men. Stephen did great wonders and miracles and certain ones in the synagogue with indignity, persuaded people to lie about Stephen. **Acts 6:11-13: *"Then they secretly persuaded some men to say, 'We have heard Stephen speak blasphemous words against Moses and against God.' So they stirred up the people and the elders and the teachers of the law. They seized Stephen and brought him before the Sanhedrin. They produced false witnesses, who testified, 'This fellow never stops speaking against this holy place and against the law.'"*** Just as had been done with Jesus, they purposely misconstrued what Stephen said. In the courtroom, Stephen's face was as an angel. He summarized the history of Israel. The summary can be read in chapter 7 in the Book of Acts. The council listened, but when Stephen spoke of Jesus, they screamed and covered their eyes. Stephen was then thrown out of the city and stoned to death. While being stoned, before his death, Stephen prayed and asked God to forgive them.

---

Men of Israel's Lies: The people were scattered abroad preaching the Word of God. There were many healed and delivered from unclean spirits. There was great joy in the city of Samaria, but a man called Simon, through sorcery, bewitched the people. They thought he was great in power. **Acts 8:10: *"and all the people, both high and low, gave him their attention and exclaimed, 'This man is rightly called the Great Power of God.'"*** They believed this lie for some time because of the work of sorcery. Through the preaching of the kingdom of God and the name of Jesus Christ, men and women were saved and baptized, including Simon. Simon believed, but wondered how the miracles and signs were done. He actually offered money, thinking he could purchase the power of God. Although he believed, his heart was not right in the sight of God.

A woman possessed with a spirit of divination, a fortune teller, followed Paul, grieving him. This woman made a great amount of money for her owners. Paul commanded the spirit in her to come out in the name of Jesus Christ. Immediately, the spirit was gone. When her owners saw that their hope to make much money was now gone, they caught Paul and Silas and falsely accused them before the civil officers. **Acts 16:20-21:** *"They brought them before the magistrates and said, 'These men are Jews, and are throwing our city into an uproar by advocating customs unlawful for us Romans to accept or practice.'"* Based on lies, Paul and Silas were beaten and imprisoned.

*Although he believed, his heart was not right with God.*

Paul's visit created an uproar in the city of Jerusalem. Numerous rumors and false accusations were said of Paul and his ministry. **Acts 21:28:** *"shouting, 'Fellow Israelites, help us! This is the man who teaches everyone everywhere against our people and our law and this place. And besides, he has brought Greeks into the temple and defiled this holy place.'"*

Approximately forty men together made a vow to eat nothing until they killed Paul. They plotted and lied in an attempt to do just that. **Acts 23:15:** *"Now then, you and the Sanhedrin petition the commander to bring him [Paul] before you on the pretext of wanting more accurate information about his case. We are ready to kill him before he gets here."* Their plot to summon Paul under false pretenses, lying in wait to kill him, was foiled.

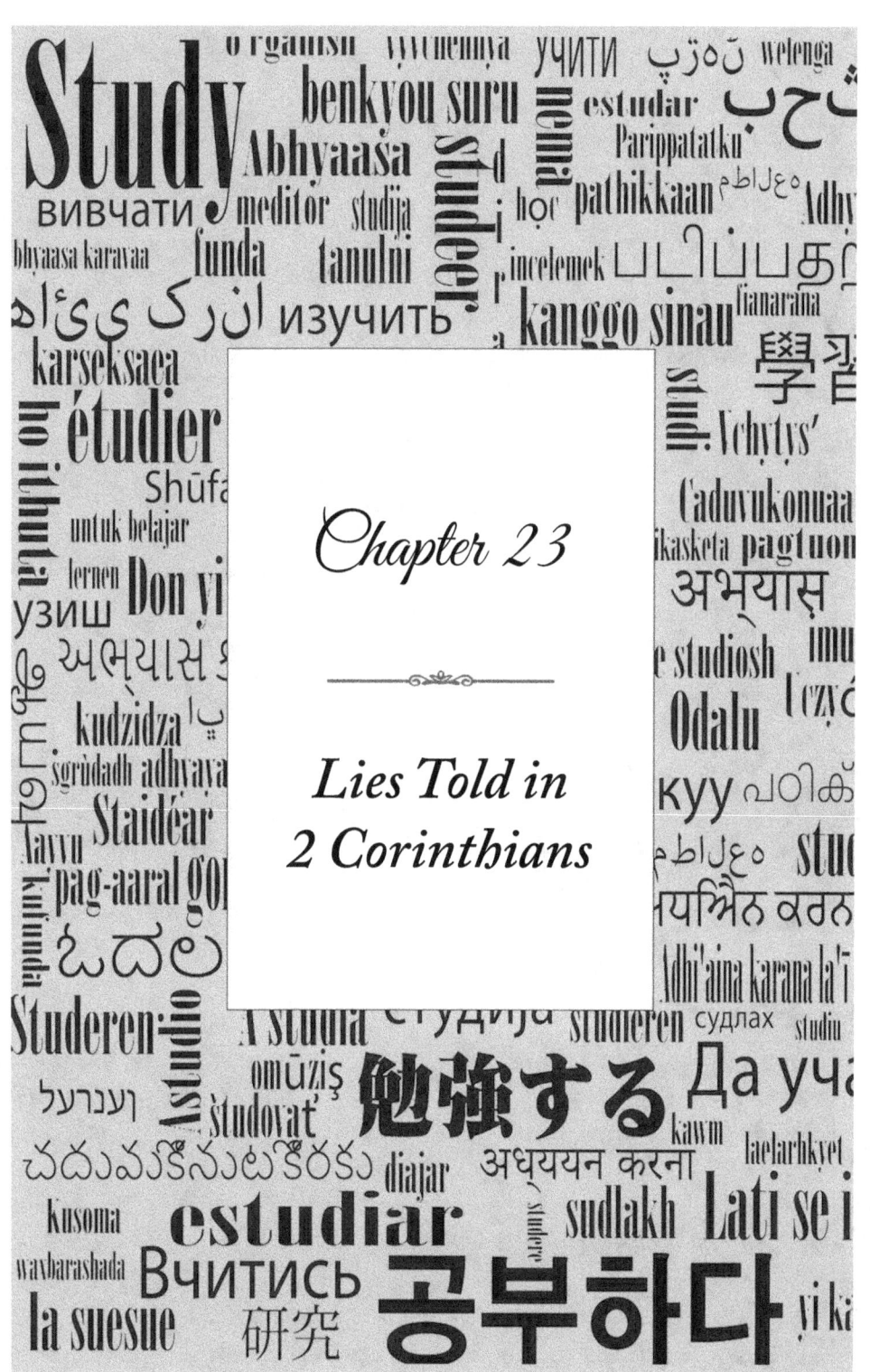

# Chapter 23

## Lies Told in 2 Corinthians

*How do you react when lies are told about you?*

The People's Lie: Paul himself tells what some had said about him and his letters. **2 Corinthians 10:10:** ***"For some say, 'His letters are weighty and forceful, but in person he is unimpressive and his speaking amounts to nothing.'"*** "They" told this lie to deceive others so they would not believe what Paul preached; they had ulterior motives. Even today, proclaiming any other name causes no trembling like the name of Jesus Christ.

# Afterword

**Lies and Consequences**

Most people, to some extent, are aware of the sexual sins that are affirmed abominations to the Lord; yet not many are even vaguely aware the Bible also says that *"lying lips are an abomination to the Lord"* (Proverbs 12:22).

Two important questions for us to consider:

1. Do we lie from fear and reverence of other people?
2. Or do we speak the truth out of fear and reverence for God?

No one is expected to change erroneous ways totally on their own. Entrust your life to Jesus Christ and allow your Maker to mold you. The God who made you knows how to fix you. This fact is true about those who truly believe, or not. Fact: Jesus Christ never lied. If He did lie, nonbelievers would surely have recorded so in historical writings. Jesus Christ lived truthfully—and truthfully, He lived. And still lives. The events of His life are documented, historical truths. To say Jesus did not live is as ludicrous as someone saying *you* never lived. Historian eyewitnesses of different faiths and nonbelievers have recorded the facts that occurred in Jesus' life. They knew He existed and knew His life events were factual—but some failed, and continue to fail, to believe He is the Son of God.

What do you believe? To be a Christian simply means to be Christlike. We are to try to emulate Him and reveal His truth to others.

Throughout this book, God uncovers Satan's most subtle trick that is damnatory and can damage even those who profess to be Christians. It starts with Satan's deception that lying is only a subtle sin. This is Satan's—the father of lies—grandest lie. Lies are the abominable sin that manifests, spreads, and leads to innumerable additional sins. A lie begets lies. Even nonbelievers agree that this is true and expect integrity from all—then why wouldn't God?

We who profess belief in God the Father, Jesus Christ the Son, and the Holy Spirit—yet are habitual liars—show that our professed faith is not true faith; and we are not bound for Heaven, but are condemned justly for our sins. Satan also believes and trembles, and his and our rebellion eternally separates us from God.

As believers, we must remain truthful and not lie; we must be honest and despise lies. Many have lied wickedly for financial gain and have seemingly prospered; but it will only be for a season, as exposure eventually comes. We are continually made privy of examples throughout the news media of liars and their subsequent consequences, downfalls, and punishment. Nevertheless, there is also much we don't see. For example, the discernment or insight that many have suffered an early death due to lies. There is always a price to pay, according to the motive of each lie.

## Accepting God's Correction

Do you feel ashamed when convicted (declared guilty) by God? If so, it means you are loved by God who is correcting you. Also, it means you love God and believe His Word. Even in our sin God will love us, keep us, and correct us; yet consequences remain. God hates lies. Lies have destructive powers, and God wants to protect you from the destructive snares of lies. God knows the destruction you will ultimately face; self-inflicted destruction, as it is our own choice to speak lies. Consequences are occurring in our lives because of lies (ours and others)—yet many are deceived into thinking they are "getting away with" their wicked lies; unaware certain destruction in their lives is imminent.

Could people very well be habitual liars and quite possibly the only ones who are not aware of it? Certainly those around them are already aware. If we believe God's Word is total truth, we must accept that we, as liars, will not get to where we call heaven. But we must also accept that God forgives, and now that you are knowledge-abled, you can change— today, right now.

## Transformation

One purpose of this book is now fulfilled—to make readers aware of the lies told in the Bible and how each liar's motives determine the consequences. An unrepentant, habitual liar possesses a characteristic of someone who is not a born-again believer. Work on your own unbelief— truly repent, truly believe, and truly receive salvation. For those who desire true transformation and change to eradicate lives of constant lying, there is hope.

Receive the free gift of grace from God and do not feel condemned when you turn in the direction you should go and stay on that path, never turning back. It's called repentance—turning away from sin and never going back to it. God's grace is truly sufficient while you are in the process of "getting it right." We are never condemned when we seek the righteousness of God. Thank God for His amazing gift of grace.

God has a written plan in the Bible to help all who seek Him in sincerity—you will find Him. Transformation comes immediately, but the changes may take one day at a time. Refuse to lie, one breath at a time. As you change, your circumstances also change. It's a process. You have the knowledge through God's Word to stop lying and gain eternal life with the Lord. God's Word forever stands.

*"The truth will set you free"*—these words were spoken by Jesus (John 8:32). If you study and believe the Bible is the Word of God, then you will learn what must be done to gain eternal life. Be amazed at the new and free "you."

## Eternal Truth

We exist in a period of time when biblical accuracy has been well-documented. Yet, God requires we must believe by faith. For instance, a virgin birth was seemingly preposterous until medical scientists were able to achieve this through implanting. Now it doesn't seem so impossible for God. In Isaiah 40:21-22, written 2,700 years ago, the Word of God states the world is round, but who listened? Throughout history there have been innumerable attempts to prove inaccuracy in the Bible—until a philosopher, scientist, archeologist, or time itself would substantiate its truth. Why do some wait for science to prove God is all-knowing? Some scientists know some things, but God knows all.

There are numerous beliefs and opinions regarding what is the truth of eternal life. Many believe the Bible is truthfully words from God, written through men—just as God has always used people to provide natural results supernaturally. There are some who express belief, yet waver about believing there is only one way and one truth to eternal life (John 14:6). Could the Bible be accurate about everything except this? I think not. One truth everyone agrees on is that all people will surely die one day—then we'll know the truth.

## Life's Manual

As cited throughout this book and throughout the Bible, God disciplines the Jews, His chosen people, for their sins; because that is true, what kind of delusive or prideful thinking has caused non-Jews to believe they are exempt from such discipline when they sin? We must study the grace of God to get an accurate understanding of His discipline. God forgives, and His hand remains out-stretched to each of us. Yet and still, there are always repercussions for our sins. And yes, the repercussions are sometimes remote or indirect. Certainly it is not beneficial for humankind that anyone repeatedly "gets away with" wrongdoing; every civil society has laws that must be followed or chaos would ensue. This universal mandate applies whether someone believes or disbelieves. Nevertheless, God's grace still abounds!

Loosen Satan's lasso from around your neck and speak the truth always! You will no longer remain blinded from the truth regarding lies. Satan's grand lie that habitual liars can still have eternal life is a deadly deception. Not to you who has spoken a lie to deflect danger, but to you habitual liars being coerced into wickedness by your master, the father of lies.

Everyone deserves an opportunity to improve and have a better life. With great hope, this book will incite you to read the Bible, Life's Manual, and achieve the life God designed especially for you! Life is lived at its best when you read the Manual. And who wouldn't want to read the all-time, best-selling Book ever written! The Bible continues to powerfully change lives after all these centuries.

What is the reason many fear reading the Bible? Have no more fear. In the Bible, God has an answer for every question you may have about life, love, relationships, career choices, parenting—every possible circumstance. Change your life to the predestined life God purposed for you. Yes, you can. You are now aware of the subtle trick the devil had up his sleeve to try to remain the master of your soul forever. Turn to God for help. You have obtained this information because God wants to help you resolve every situation, truthfully. God wants you to have eternal life with Him—He desires no one to perish.

## No Liars in Heaven

Jesus knows when you are truly His; when calling and depending on the name of Jesus the Christ, you can depart from iniquity. Throughout the Word of God and on to the very end in Revelation, it states that liars will not go to heaven. Many may be inclined to ignore the costs associated with lying and ignore the clarion instructions from the Word of God regarding lying. But I urge you to turn to the last pages of the Holy Bible and read about the severity of lies. Be blessed by reading the truth. *God wants to safeguard you from the self-destruction of lies.* (Words worth repeating, and words worth rereading.)

God is not mocked, jeer not; God is a righteous Judge. Our ultimate Judge is also a just Judge. As told in 1 Kings 3:21-28, both mothers were prostitutes, but they were not equally judged by Solomon, or by God. One of the mothers was exposed as a liar. God says we should abhor lies. If lying is a seemingly acceptable solution to achieving what we need or want in life—expect a dark end.

Human beings need to seek and secure a kinship connection to God through Jesus Christ to understand and know ourselves with depth. We consist of soul, body, and spirit. Without accessibility to the true and living God—who is Spirit and Creator of your spirit—a vital entity of your being is latent.

Your spirit (sometimes referred to as your heart, though not the physical heart) is your true self, housed by your body. Seek to know and to grow the deeper you. Obtain guidance from the preeminent wisdom of God through His Word—the Bible. Worship God in spirit and in truth. Study the Bible to show yourself approved and not ashamed. This is the way to live. This is the way to life.

Patricia Von Johnson

# WRITE THE TRUTH

# WRITE THE TRUTH

Patricia Von Johnson

# WRITE THE TRUTH

# WRITE THE TRUTH

Patricia Von Johnson

# WRITE THE TRUTH

# WRITE THE TRUTH

# Appendix

**Lies, Liars, and Lying in Scripture**

In the Bible, there are numerous verses of Scripture that speak specifically about lies, liars, and lying. A Bible concordance is a great source to easily find any particular word, topic, name, or place. A concordance helps you find exactly where most anything is located in the Bible. Concordances are extremely helpful for research, which will lead you to many interesting truths throughout the Bible.

Examples of Scriptures citing lies, liars, and lying:

Psalm 58:3 – *Even from birth the wicked go astray; from the womb they are wayward, spreading lies.*

Psalm 101:7 – *…no one who speaks falsely will stand in my presence.*

Psalm 119:29 – *Keep me from deceitful ways….*

Psalm 119:69 – *Though the arrogant have smeared me with lies….*

Psalm 119:163 – *I hate and detest falsehood….*

Psalm 120:2 – *Save me, Lord, from lying lips and from deceitful tongues.* Proverbs 6:16-17 – *There are six things the Lord hates…a lying tongue….* Proverbs 12:22 – *The Lord detests lying lips….*

Proverbs 13:5 – *T"e righteous hate what is false….*

Proverbs 19:9 – *A false witness will not go unpunished, and whoever pours out lies will perish.*

Proverbs 19:22 – *…better to be poor than a liar.*

Proverbs 21:6 – *A fortune made by a lying tongue is a fleeting vapor and a deadly snare.*

Proverbs 30:6 – *Do not add to his words, or he will rebuke you and prove you a liar.*

Isaiah 28:15 – *…We have made a lie our refuge and falsehood our hiding place.*

Isaiah 28:17 – *…justice…and righteousness…will sweep away the refuge, the lie, and water will overflow your hiding place.*

Isaiah 32:7 – *Scoundrels use wicked methods, they make up evil schemes to destroy the poor with lies….*

Isaiah 59:13 – *…uttering lies our hearts have conceived.*

Isaiah 63:8 – *…Surely they are my people, children who will be true to me….* Jeremiah 7:8 – *But look, you are trusting in deceptive words that are worthless.* Jeremiah 9:5 – *…They have taught their tongue to lie….*

Hosea 4:2 – *There is only cursing, lying and murder, stealing….*

Hosea 10:13 – *…you have reaped evil, you have eaten the fruit of deception….*

Zechariah 13:3 – *…You have told lies in the Lord's name….*

Romans 1:25 – *They exchanged the truth about God for a lie….*

Galatians 1:20 – *I assure you before God that what I am writing you is no lie.*

Colossians 3:9 – *Do not lie to each other….*

1 Timothy 4:2 – *Such teachings come through hypocritical liars....*

Titus 1:2 – *...which God, who does not lie....*

James 3:14 – *...do not boast about it or deny the truth.*

1 John 1:6 – *If we claim to have fellowship with him and yet walk in the darkness, we lie and do not live out the truth.*

1 John 2:4 – *Whoever says, "I know him," but does not do what he commands is a liar, and the truth is not in that person.*

1 John 4:20 – *Whoever claims to love God yet hates a brother or sister is a liar....*

Revelation 21:8 – *...and all the liars—they will be consigned to the fiery lake....*

# About the Author

Patricia Von Johnson, a former entrepreneur, returned to college at the age of 50 to study Theology. She recently graduated Cum Laude from Trinity International University. She is the proud mother of one daughter, Qiana, who graduated from college just one week apart from her mother.

For the past twenty years, Patricia has traveled the world as an international flight attendant with American Airlines. Her global adventures include an African safari in Kenya, climbing the active Volcano de Pacaya in Guatemala, and Baptism in the Jordan River in Israel.

Mentoring is her mission—her efforts combine the Lighthouse Community Church Adopt-a-School program and the Take Stock in Children program. A prior Board Member of the Mental Health Association of Dade County "Listen to Children" program, she also taught Children's Church at Upper Room Ministries. Patricia resides in South Florida.

Please contact the author by email at:

patricia@LiestoldintheBible.com

www.ingramcontent.com/pod-product-compliance
Lightning Source LLC
Chambersburg PA
CBHW052144110526
44591CB00012B/1854